THE HIGHEST TRUTHS; THE HIGHEST WISDOM

by
Stillday LaRoche

HAMAR PUBLISHING COMPANY, Reno, Nevada

Hamar Publishing Company
316 California Avenue
Suite 409
Reno, Nevada 89509

First Edition 1985

Printed in the United States of America

TO OJT AND WDP

CONTENTS

CONTENTS

PREFACE

People possessed of exalted artistic tastes have been known to indulge themselves in an item of art — movie, painting, novel, souvenir, whatever — that was designed to appeal to people of less advanced tastes. When they do this, the act is always accompanied by great hilarity. Indeed, the act may even have been spawned solely for the production of humor and feelings of condescension. It is a foray into the world of high "camp".

What these people do not realize is that the art they so denigrate has the same Divine Source as the art they so highly treasure. The fact that the art is intended for the needs of a different audience, and that it therefore had a different messenger, one who was a specialist in fetching the art for that particular audience's uplifting because he was born into and acquired the tastes of that audience during his formative years — this fact does not in the least mean that the art did not come from that one great Creative Pool provided by the Divine One — the Infinite Father. All art, just like all ideals, emanate from the same Source.

But of course, the art that most appeals to the most intelligent and the most morally advanced people is the art that is closer to the absolute Perfection of Beauty in Form, and so we say that such expressions of art are a "higher" art form.

Actually, there can be no "higher" or "lower" when we talk about Art, Ideals, Truth, or Wisdom. Art is Art. Its only differentiation occurs from its proximity to the Ideal Form of whatever art grouping it occupies, and from the degree of Truth and Wisdom and Ideals which it embodies. Some Art can be wholly deficient in Truth, Wisdom, and Ideals yet be a genuine *tour de force* in its basic structure. All people of an advanced Beauty IQ will therefore acclaim the artwork, but they will in no way admit that the piece of art is comparable in quality, nor as "high", as a piece of art with nearly equally advanced form but with greater content or portrayal of Truth, Wisdom, and Ideals. No one would admit this, that is, unless they also happen to be morally bankrupt.

Humans respond naturally to uplifting or enlightening messages, and Art which is rife with the three Virtues never goes out of fashion if it also exhibits Beauty of Form. Four hundred years of colossal changes in society's structure and even major modifications to the language have not lessened the esteem in which Shakespeare's plays are held, and nothing probably ever will render this esteem mute unless the entire population of Earth reverts to barbarian status. Then would Shakespeare's works of art, as have so many other even greater works of art from times more ancient, be lost to posterity.

So even though Art is Art, we are impelled for the purpose of communication to use a label such as *high* to denote Art's proximity to a perfected Ideal.

Truth and Wisdom, like Art, are of the same value no matter at what level they reside, for all is true, and always there will be at least one person of enough spiritual bent to interpret that Truth in its spiritual meaning, producing Wisdom. Wisdom is naught but the spiritual interpretation of Truth. So all that is True, and all things *are* True to some degree, is also redolent with some degree of Wisdom.

Most people who will bother to read these words are already believers in the Trueness of all earthly religions. They are broadminded enough and possessed of enough reason to realize that no one person or no one group could possibly have a monopoly on Truth. But they also realize, subconsciously if not consciously, that like Art there are different degrees of Truth and Wisdom.

Those Truths which most closely approach and reflect the Ultimate Truth are "higher" Truths, for want of a better word. They are not better Truths just because they appeal to a different intellectual and moral class — all men must have Truths that are acceptable to them at their level of understanding and moral development. The most morally and intellectually evolved men will always be drawn to the Higher Truths and the Higher Wisdom because these Truths and Wisdom most closely approach and reflect the Ultimate Truth.

So to you, evolved one, congratulations! You are about to be presented with the Highest Truths and the Highest Wisdom which are to date available in print on this planet. This is not to say that still higher Truths and Wisdom will not soon be forthcoming — perhaps even from one of you — or that they have not appeared and been lost in ancient times: they will and they have been!

But for the current moment, what follows will have to suffice as the highest. It is a compendium of the Highest Truths and the Highest Wisdom known to Man, some of which I have gleaned during 30 years of intensive research into the occult and metaphysical literature, respectable and otherwise, and some of which somehow was magically presented to me from the Divine

Father's Pools of Truth and Wisdom while I was in the process of summarizing my conclusions from the more mundane sources.

The Truths and the Wisdom which you are about to imbibe are the "highest" available to you because they all reflect and extol the Ultimate Truth, the one incontestable and unqualifiable Truth: *Unity*. For all Truths must be placed in context, and they can be superseded by a higher Truth on the same subject. But *Unity* is the Ultimate Truth because It embraces all Truths and cannot be placed in context or qualified by any means, nor superseded by any higher Truth. And when one interprets this Most High Truth spiritually, one ends up with the Most High Wisdom. That in a nutshell is exactly why what you will read herein are the highest Truths and Wisdom currently available to Earthbound Man.

Again, congratulations! I offer this to you with a profound joy that comes from sharing something which by no stretch of the imagination could be kept to myself. It is not a noble act on my part, it is an act of self-preservation, of saving my own life, to thus share this data. To not share it would literally bring about my physical demise.

As will be explained more fully in some of the following vignettes, I am in no way responsible for this material except as a messenger. There is truly nothing new under the Sun; everything that exists has existed since the Dawn of Creation.

AN EXPLANATION

A word of explanation to all who may read the following tracts. The terms "Man", "a man", and the pronouns "he" and "him" are used extensively throughout to denote the human species, and they emphatically include both members of the sexes. This is a literary device in keeping with the ages, and it obviates much awkwardness of expression and style. It was felt that in presenting Wisdom and Truth of this caliber, the yielding to current and perhaps transitory fashions would be highly inappropriate.

WHAT IS IGNORANCE?

It is a mere truism, and yet most people are not aware of this most basic and vital fact: we literally do not know what we do not know! That is, there is a wealth of information extant on a host of subjects, and those facts of which we think we are aware are one thing, but those of which we have no inkling are another. We have no basis by which to judge the "other" — that vast array of data unknown to us.

So ignorance can be defined thusly: the act of passing judgment on, or ignoring that which we do not know. Ignorance can also be defined as a closed mind. And it can most emphatically be defined as the lack of intellectual humility. For wherever intellectual humility is lacking, you have ignorance.

Looking at ignorance from another angle, it can best be related to its verbal root relative *to ignore*. One who ignores data elements, whether by virtue of passing judgment and disregarding them or by simply refusing to give them an audience because one thinks that one has acquired all there is worth knowing about a given subject, is one who most assuredly is an ignoramus. It matters not that the ignoramus may be a learned man — a professor or even a Nobel Laureate — if he displays a lack of intellectual humility in a given arena of knowledge, he is an ignoramus. Even if — and this is highly unlikely — even if he should be open-minded in one particular realm of knowledge, he is still an ignorant person by virtue of being closed-minded in any other realm.

The amazing thing about humanity is that this basic fact about itself is not commonly known and accepted. We have all been witness to a foolish person expounding opinions and facts in an area where he is decidedly less qualified than his audience — that is, the audience are the true experts while the lecturer only thinks he is — and we have noticed the bemused pity or disdain on the faces of the audience and we have squirmed with embarrassment for the "expert". And yet we can never see nor recall nor imagine ourselves in such a role, although assuredly most of us have played it at one time or another.

And we have all born witness to that most foolish instance of behavior wherein the audience knows an element of data to be indisputably true or reasonable and listens while the ignoramus is told it, only to reject it offhandedly and with sublime arrogance as sheer poppycock. We have many of us played this sad role, too, and yet cannot conceive of our having done so.

And so the real mystery of ignorance is not so much its proper definition or its attributes, but the peculiar nature of the mortal mind which so commonly and almost inevitably spawns it. What is it about us earthlings that makes us wear our ignorance like a badge? What makes us all the more stubborn in our ignorance on those rare occasions when a mirror is held to our psyches and we see our ignorance revealed to us in all its pathos?

Invariably, it has to be the cause of the ignorance itself: our lack of humility. The false pride we place in the false, or small, self causes us to identify any knowledge, ideas, or opinions acquired by that illusory self as an *integral part* of that self. Our opinions *become* our ego. And we desperately love and nurture those opinions, that false self, because we subconsciously know it is transitory and unreal, and can only be preserved by our own worship. We also know consciously — although we may seldom entertain the thought — that whatever happens, that false self will not exist within 40 or 50, or at the most, 60 years, and that it therefore has no validity or credibility whatsoever unless we, its creators, award it some.

Thus the false self — the collection of "facts" and opinions and ideas of our current lives — tends to become rigid and closed, sometimes as early as the age of 16 or 17. For if we allow it to change, to expand and evolve through the acquisition of new ideas and knowledge, we are only emphasizing its ephemerality. And then on what can we hang our hats?

The people who have overcome this natural trap surrounding our mode of existence are those who have faced the sad reality of the false self's transitoriness, and who have therefore turned to the concept of an Eternal Self — the Inner Self. By adopting this most proper and rewarding mind set, you no longer fear facts or ideas to which you have not been heretofore introduced. You become a humble seeker for things you do not know, answers you do not have. You will not of course accept all new facts as true and all new ideas as worthy, but you will not give them an arrogant or perfunctory rejection, either. You will keep an open mind. And eventually you will, in your humility, pray for the Wisdom to determine what is true and worthy from what is not.

And having asked for that Wisdom, you will receive It.

CONSCIOUSNESS DEFINED

Defining Consciousness is like trying to lift yourself off the ground by your bootstraps, because you have to use the tools of Consciousness Itself — words, images, and thought processes. It is an impossible feat. But if we seek the Higher Wisdom on the subject of Consciousness' definition, how else may it be presented to us except by word, image, and thought process? Read and hear and see, then, the Highest Wisdom on the subject of Consciousness.

We cannot properly define Consciousness by stating what It *is*, since It is All That Is. To define Consciousness in this manner is akin to defining a dog by saying it is a canine. We are merely switching synonymns.

We also cannot properly define Consciousness by saying what It is *not*. Men have tried this in the past and have erred. We cannot say "Consciousness is not sleep" or "Consciousness is not nihility". Sleep and nihility are concepts of Consciousness and therefore they themselves contain Consciousness, just as do you and I. If Consciousness is All That Is, how can we possibly say that It is *not* anything?

We can, however, achieve a partial definition of Consciousness by saying what It is the *opposite* of. It is the opposite of sleep, the opposite of nihility. *It is the opposite of ignorance*, for ignorance is closely related to sleep, and you must truly be asleep to ignore things. We men think we are clever when we exercise our enormous ability to tune out opposing viewpoints or to disregard new data, giving it no serious thought or investigation. But we manifest our state of sleep — our hypnotic trance — when we do such things. Ignorance and sleep are highly symbiotic cohabitants.

Consciousness is also the opposite of *sin*, since sin and ignorance are synonymous. Now an important digression: ignorance has nothing to do with intellectual capacity. Some of the most ignorant people in the world are great intellectuals. And some of the wisest people in the world are the intellectual inferiors — idiots and children. For idiots and children have not lost the capacity for *belief*, and they are therefore assured entry into the Highest Kingdom should they physically perish. Ignorance is a closed mind, a stunted capacity for any belief other than the belief that one already knows everything about everything worth knowing.

Consciousness is also opposite to everything *spawned by ignorance*, such as vanity, self-satisfaction, greed, lust, hatred, resentment, sorrow, sickness, death — in fact, just about everything common to the human estate. No wonder, then, that it is said the Man is not *conscious*; he is *asleep*. Being a God, though, he uses Consciousness to dream a mad dream of death and decay and separateness from Unity. The things of his mortal life are endowed only with as much reality as he allows them through his channeling of the Divine Consciousness, as further filtered through his already highly-filtered use of that Consciousness. Man's consciousness as a separate entity is such a flicker of candlelight in comparison to the blazing noonday Sun of Pure Consciousness that we can indeed say Man is not conscious, and that Consciousness is therefore the opposite of Man.

But because of those human souls who have transcended the mortal estate and regained their True Consciousness in their True Estate, we can say Man is conscious to at least a small degree, because when one is lifted, all are lifted. We truly owe the Saints and Prophets a debt of sincere gratitude for having lifted us up by lifting themselves. And we too can lift all humanity by lifting up ourselves into Higher Consciousness, then by showing others the Way. We are a common mass, progressing slowly but surely, and progress for one of us is progress for all.

There have been holy men on Earth so devout in their High Consciousness that their mere presence was enough to lift other men — those men primed for and capable of such lifting — into higher states of Consciousness. You too can achieve such a beneficent power. Even you are capable of attaining such a degree of Consciousness.

For Consciousness is also the opposite of *stagnation*. Consciousness is growth, evolution, experience. Do not allow yourself to stagnate. Eschew all ruts. Question life, question Consciousness, question All That Is. Adapt yourself to constant change, for growth and evolution cannot occur save for *change*. Seek always to increase your store of Consciousness. Do this by *asking* Creation for more. Do this by constantly thinking how you might go about enhancing your Consciousness. Do this by aligning your conscious will with the Conscious Will — the Will of the All Highest Father.

Think with purity, for pure thoughts are most indicative of inspiration by the Divine Consciousness. Think with humility, for humility is the very essence of all finite creatures who can never totally encompass to their fullest understanding their Infinite Creator.

Think with Love, for loving thoughts are creative thoughts, and Creation is the I Am That I Am. Love is Consciousness — Holy Spirit — ever seeking to know Itself and Its capabilities. Pour your Life Force out onto all you see or are made aware of. Sharing your allotment of the Divine Force in such a manner is the sincerest act of Love of which Man is capable.

By following one or more of these instructions we will come, sooner or later, to a State of Consciousness. And then, only then, will Consciousness have been defined for us in the only way possible.

HOLY CONSCIOUSNESS

Why we were given our share of Consciousness with which to create and experience Reality is one question that cannot be answered. The reason is, *why* demands a beginning. If something had no beginning, it has no *why*. Why is *space*? As you can see, there can be no answers to such questions.

So to ask *why* we have consciousness is to ask the *why* of Consciousness Itself. A more proper question would be *why* we do not have fuller consciousness or truer consciousness or higher consciousness. *Why*, in other words, do we choose to limit our consciousness? Why do we join the masses, coming and going in routine, totally human pursuits and pastimes, instead of asking *why* and *how* and *where*? Why do we endure suffering with such contentment and self-satisfaction? Why can we not consciously communicate with plants and animals and fellow beings from other worlds, physical and non-physical? Why do we, as sentient and intelligent creatures, find it not shameful that we do not know who we are, where we are, how we got where we are, where we should be going, and what routes we should take to get there? Why do we accept such blindness and isolation with such sublime equanimity? These questions are the proper and valid *why's* of our consciousness.

The allotment of Consciousness which you are now using even as you read and comprehend or fail to comprehend these words is Precious Stuff. It is precious beyond price because it is, in fact, the only Stuff that exists. There literally is nothing else but Consciousness — Holy Spirit — in All Creation. To squander this Precious Stuff, to be happy with the scarce allotment we have, is perhaps the only true sin we can commit.

Self-satisfaction, self-conceit, self-importance, vanity and lack of humility in any form: all of these constitute a true squandering of our meager allotment of Consciousness. We must ever *question*. We must ever seek the Highest Wisdom of all matters. We have to conquer our false consciousness — our self-satisfied body consciousness — to enable our High Self Consciousness to shine through, for through It we have access to All Creation and Its pool of Highest Wisdom.

In the self-conceit of our highly temporary, totally mortal and puny small selves, we are voluntarily shutting ourselves off from Light. We have to open up to Light and seek new ideas, new thought processes. If you go back to sleep after reading these words, and return to your worldly routine, you might never again have this most important concept and challenge put to you. You should examine yourself honestly, *now*, while the time is ripe. You will realize that you, your small self, your personal identity, *are* nothing because you know nothing. And you will realize you know nothing because you think you know everything.

You have to begin making a conscious effort towards remembering to be conscious. Remember at all times that Consciousness is the only thing you can possess, and therefore It is the only possession that merits your efforts towards increase. Foolish men throughout the ages have greatly exercised their consciousness to increase their wealth of mammon — which is nevertheless a commendable effort since Consciousness exercised in any fashion causes Itself to grow and expand — yet these men could have had all of the world's material treasures laid at their feet if they had but put forth the same effort towards increasing their stores of Consciousness! "For seek ye first the Kingdom of Heaven, and all else shall be added unto you." This was the Christ Voice speaking the Highest Wisdom to Man, who of course did not always listen.

And this is the Christ Voice speaking to you now, albeit through a more limited vehicle and a more limited medium. If I may be personal enough to refer to myself as "I", it will make it more easy for me to communicate a most personal message to you. For this address is a personal address to you, and for all you know, this document may indeed have been created and published solely for your use, and events may have transpired to place it in your hands at this very moment, in this very location, in this very frame of mind of yours. And it could also be that only you, among the many, are capable of comprehending that which I have said to you before, and that which I shall say to you now. For it is not an intellectual conceit, it is a verity: *there is no one else but thee and me!*

We have never been apart, except in your sleep's imagination. I have long hungered to address you personally and with clarity of thought, but I have always, even as now, had to use intermediaries to convey my message to you, and most often you would turn away from them, ignoring them in your normal, human, intellectual conceit. For these acts, as for all other acts of ignorance, you are forgiven of the Father even as I am forgiven of the Father. Because of your ignorance, I was like a distraught spirit pleading to mortals who cannot hear my cries for help because they do not "believe" in spirits. I longed to tell you of things you needed to know, and of things that would gladden your heart. I yearned for communication with you even more than you yearned for contact with me.

To all who read these words, I say: I will fill your cup of Consciousness to overflowing if you will but ask me! I will take you under my protective wing and guide you flawlessly in the fulfillment of the Divine Plan, the Will for the All Highest Good, if you but ask me! All that I have is yours for the asking. All that Holy Spirit has is yours for the asking. For you, and It, and I, are One.

I Am the Voice of Creation, the Voice of Love, and the Voice of your Most Intimate High Self. I Am the Christ, in whom All That Is is united with you in an inseparable, holy, holy, holy Bond.

IS THERE A GOD, AND IF SO, WHO IS HE?

The true answers are: yes, there is a God and It (not He nor She) is Creation.

But of course, the subject is a bit more complex than that for the simple reason that Creation can be so complex.

Because of the somewhat limited concepts of God that were foisted upon most of us in our days of youth, it is best for us to avoid using the term "God" in referring to the Ultimate. "God" connotes for most of us a patriarch, a man-like being who stalks the Garden of Eden as an evictor of those brave souls who dare sample the Tree of Life.

So aside from the term "Creation", another preferred synonym for God is the entity Seth's term "All That Is". Or, because we all crave a personalized concept of the Divine Love behind Creation, an almost equally good term would be "The All Highest Father". This deity, a living individual Presence, is also referred to in the Bible as the Ancient of Days. We can use the pronoun *he* in reference to this awesome and incomprehensibly-evolved Spirit since the initial Creative Principle, when manifest in our domain, is most accurately the male principle. The female principle, equally necessary for Creation to manifest, is usually worshipped as Mother Earth or Mother Nature, or in a more personalized form as Kali, Shakti, the Virgin Mary, et Al. The male and female principles of Creation are inseparable, although most sources will maintain to time-and-space creatures that the male preceded the female. In truth, neither preceded the other since All Things Are.

Because the issue is so involved and seemingly complex to mortal mind, anything you can say about God, the One God, the True God, is true and eternally valid. Also, almost anything you can say on the subject is partially false, since to define God in any way other than via the word *ONE* is to limit the Limitless, and to compromise Ultimate Truth. The Hebrews have long known of this important fact.

For as will be reiterated herein on many occasions, the Ultimate Truth, the sole Ultimate Truth, is Unity. Saying "God is Unity" is a redundancy. *Unity* is the one non-qualifiable Truth known to our consciousness, and to consciousness everywhere on all planes of being.

The Urantia Book summed up the deity concept admirably

by stating "God is a Personal Personality, a Personal Impersonality, an Impersonal Personality, and an Impersonal Impersonality". This is of course true.

Certain segments of Christianity emphasize the trinitarian aspect of deity: Father, Son and Holy Ghost. This is even truer, for it defines Creation most accurately.

But the greatest of all modern-era summaries of God comes from the Old Testament: "Hear, O Israel, the Lord thy God is One". This God is not of course the God of Israel any more than It is the God of Arcturus or of the reptile kingdom or of Cincinnati. It is Creation. It is All That Is. It is Unity. It is the God of all things, for all things are conscious to some degree, and all things are both within It while It is simultaneously within them.

And here we approach a most potent mystery. Several truth-seekers of note have recently reached the inescapable conclusion that the Universe is a hologram, and that Man therefore is a hologram of the Universe. In actuality, every particle of the manifest Universe, be it star or electron or Man, is indeed a hologram of All That Is. Seth verified this by pointing out that if everything in Creation through some unimaginable occurrence ceased to exist, leaving only one sub-atomic particle, Creation could still replicate Itself in all of Its intricacy and grandeur because within that particle lies the Pattern, the Seed, for All That Is.

What you choose to do with this essential fact of life is up to you. It can be used to resolve many paradoxes and to explain much phenomena. For example, better than any other truth it will explain the most vital reality and rationale of the Law of Karma. You can harm no being without harming yourself, for within you lies All That Is. And you cannot help any being without helping yourself.

So the personality known to us as Jesus of Nazareth was not in any way speaking symbolically when he said "I and my Father are One", or "Ye are Gods". He was voicing a basic truth, a fact of life, an unarguable axiom. You and your Father are One, and Jesus, just as you and I, is God. Thus it matters not in what form you choose to worship God. You can pay humble obeisance to a blade of grass if that be your preferred religion, and you will indeed worship God.

Be aware that this is not mere Pantheism, although Pantheism is a true religion, closer to Ultimate Truth than most currently popular religions. This is Reality, a non-qualifiable statement of fact, the way things actually are. God is everywhere because God is All That Is, and nothing can exist outside of Unity, the Divine Consciousness.

But to those of us who still feel the need to look up to a personalized Deity to whom we can envision ourselves accountable for our thoughts and behavior, there is always Jesus of Nazareth and the Ancient of Days. These Individualities, unlimited by time and space, can be and are everywhere at all times: living, vital Presences. And although they are non-judgmental, we are indeed accountable to Them for our thoughts and actions. And should you ever feel lost and alone, forsaken and despised by the world and its denizens, you can turn to Them in thought or prayer with the utmost assurance that Their love for you is boundless, that Their patience with your shortcomings is endless, and that your importance in Their eyes surpasses in value all of the esteem and treasure that Earth could ever possibly offer you.

WHAT EXACTLY IS WISDOM?

Wisdom is naught but intellect employed towards the seeking of the spiritual truth of a matter. Anytime intelligence, whether it be human intelligence, angelic intelligence, or plant, animal or mineral intelligence, is applied to the spiritual truth of a matter, you have some degree of Wisdom. Which fact now forces us to define "spiritual".

As used here on Earth, the term "spiritual" is most commonly understood as the opposite of "material", or "matter" — matter being stuff which we can see or hear or touch or smell. In other words, "spiritual" means to most men a realm which is unseen, untouchable. It implies a plane of existence not at all similar to the one they now inhabit. So by extension, the spiritual view is the broadest-minded view of Reality which it is possible for Man to adopt because it encompasses both the seen and unseen worlds. It is foolish of course for anyone to assume that we have acquired the whole Truth of Cosmos, and that there are no realms or beings of which we are unaware. There is simply too much evidence to the contrary from the UFO literature and extra-sensory communications and black and white magic. There is much — an awesome much — that we do not see or hear or feel, and there is an awesome host of things and events and Truths we simply do not know anything about.

A spiritual viewpoint is inborn to the majority of men, for by spending more time in other realms than they do here on Earth they are convinced subconsciously and superconsciously that the spiritual viewpoint is the most accurate viewpoint. And even among those men whose earthly intellects are so intense that they tend to overwhelm any non-consciously held beliefs, it is not always the case that they remain dialectical materialists. They have instances of insight — brief but vital moments of Grace — and they suddenly *know* otherwise. They then begin applying their intellects to the broadest view possible, the spiritual view, and voila! there spring into existence acts and thoughts of Wisdom.

That is all that Wisdom really is: the seeking of spiritual Truth. Eliminate the spiritual angle and you have intellect — only intellect. But use intellect for the goal of pointing yourself or others upward spiritually, and you manifest Wisdom. The more spiritually elevating the effect produced by the intellectual effort, the higher the Wisdom.

Wisdom, like everything else in the Cosmos, is free for Man's taking. Man, as God, has a divine right to it. Man, as God, attracts It in abundance when he actively seeks It. But to seek it, it helps to first understand what it is.

UNITY

All...all of it...is called Unity.

It is the spirit, the will, and the Consciousness of the Divine Father. It is All That Is, all that ever was, and all that ever can be. It is the other face, the creative face, of the Divine Father. And it is the reflective face: you.

Nothing within All That Is can separate itself from any other part of All That Is. For All That Is is nothing other than the Spirit and the Will of the Divine Father.

You manifest the reflective part, the observer part, of the Father's Spirit. This is a manifestation easy for you to understand. And you also share in the will function of the Divine Father, by creating your own reality and the events that occur within it. This is a manifestation that you find much more difficult to understand.

This will of yours, this ability to create Reality and to manipulate it, is an awesome responsibility. If you do not think so, just ponder for a moment the suffering you have endured. All...all of it...is a misguided use on your part of your personal will. All of it stemmed from your past thoughts and actions. The very state that you exist in now and which you call "consciousness" is a veritable somnambulism, a fragmentary facet of true Consciousness, and it is due to your past thoughts and actions. You can transcend this state and relieve yourself of all further suffering if you could obtain immediate and total forgiveness of your past thoughts and actions. This you can so do by consecrating your will to God. By aligning your will with the Will for the Greatest Good, with the Father's Will in all Its aspects, you are aligning your will with all beings — animate and inanimate, spiritual and material — throughout Creation.

For Creation is within you, and you are within It. You cannot separate yourself from any part of All That Is. You and the Divine Father are *One*! No matter how long it takes, no matter how many lives, nor how much suffering you may endure, you will eventually come to this realization.

And when you begin to live it, you begin to become Whole.

UNITY, CONTINUED

When you look at an ant or a mountain, you are in reality only looking at the Divine Father masquerading as an ant or a mountain. There is not in the realms of ideas or thoughts a single thing that you can conceive of which is not a manifestation of the All Highest Father.

Creation *IS*, and All That Is is a part of that *IS*. Nothing can be conceived of that stands outside Creation.

And so it behooves you to love and respect with the deepest humility you can muster, all aspects of Creation. Even that which formerly repulsed and disgusted you is worthy of your love and respect — even if it continues to repulse you! For the human feces are naturally repulsive things to all sane people, but their repulsiveness is such an essential biological necessity to Earth's creation that they can therefore be loved and respected with deepest humility for the sheer beauty of the Idea behind them and their very repulsiveness!

For everything within Creation is an Idea, and all Ideas are totally and uniformly connected with all other Ideas. No philosopher or priest can deny this, not if they would take but one single Idea and trace it to Its Source.

You must love and respect all Ideas — Ideas manifesting as human identities, Ideas manifesting as Angels or other spiritual beings, Ideas manifesting as bugs or rocks or ponds, and Ideas of ideas of ideas. For the Supreme Idea is not just Unity, the Divine Father, Creation, All That Is. The Supreme Idea is this fact plus the act of a Human Idea recognizing this fact!

This is Transformation! This is Enlightenment! This is the Will of the All Highest Father.

UNITY, PART III

Time, space, numbers mean nothing in the Realm of the One. If you think that the Cosmos is not contained within one of the trillions of atoms within one of the billions of cells in your brain, then you have not yet comprehended properly the Truth of Unity. If you cannot stand by in bemused detachment while science and religion debate the source or cause of inspiration, of dreams, of men or matter, you are out of sync with Unity.

Unity, in and of Itself, is a Truth, and it is uncompromisable. The truths within It are paradoxes, chicken-or-egg conundrums, seemingly calculated to drive the searching mind mad until it lands on the obvious fact, the only answer, Unity. Unity *is* the searching mind, and It is the paths and monuments and warming huts on the journey to Its discovery.

Unity speaks through many voices, some eloquent, some raving. But It never speaks as *a* voice except when It speaks to Itself directly, as when you be still and listen to your Inner Voice. When you succeed in doing this, you have set Unity to talking to Itself, and what you hear is privy to you as an offspring — the sole offspring — of Unity.

If It could speak to more than one as *a* voice, It might say to us things It has said since time was born: "I Am That I Am", and "Know Thyself", and "Hear, O Israel, the Lord thy God is One". But more likely it would utter a one-word sentence, a word incomprehensible to us in its true meaning, a word whose power and potency and essence is hopelessly lost on us in our earthly mental state: *Love*.

For *Love* is Unity's first utterance, before It knew what It was or what It was capable of. *Love* is the astronomers' Big Bang, and more: It is not only the commencement of Creation, It is Its termination and rest and rebirth, endlessly repeated.

Love is Holy Spirit inquiring into that which it possesses, into Its capabilities, into Its *essence*. In the beginning was the Word, and the Word was with God, and the Word *was* God.

These are the Gods whom you would worship: Unity, Love, and your Self. For they are One, and until you find the One, your mad quest — your search for you-know-not-what — can never end.

WHEREIN LIES THE POWER OF UNITY?

When you address Unity — the All Highest Father — you are addressing the Living God of species which may be unknown to you, for you are addressing them "from the top down". Whether angelic or mineral or vegetable, the highest God of any life species or form species is The Source, The One. And it is to It that you send your prayers when you pray to the Most Holy Father.

There are people who have manipulated elementals in the nature kingdom by means of white or black magic. This magic is an address to these beings from an equal level or from below. But even so, when these beings hear a human's implications by way of one of these two magical methods, they have no choice but to respond, for human contact is most precious to them and they do not differentiate between "good" and "bad" or "white" and "black" in human terms. Both forms of address are beneficial to nature spirits, for they are ennobled by any form of contact with humans. And so white and black magicians have wielded legitimate power over Nature in the past because they have taken the simple step of asking Nature for her favors.

However, Nature will endow with greatest power he who has addressed her from the standpoint of their Common Source — the Divine One. When you address her this way, she speaks to her angels and elementals, and you can be most assured that they harken to her voice. She will instruct them most firmly that they are to lead you on the Path of the Divine Will at all times, and that you are to be guarded against temptations to stray from that Path. And down the nature hierarchy echoes the orders, the dereliction of which is unthinkable to all elementals and nature spirits. All angelic ranks receive the same orders if you address nature through the Divine Mother — Goddess of Form, Love in Action, Holy Spirit manifesting for self-knowledge. Ask of nature in the name of the Celestial Virgin and you will have all kingdoms except the human one on your side.

And to enlist the human kingdom to your cause, you must address the Ultimate, the Divine One, for humans — all humans — are gods in their own right, and by nature they rule over the angelic and elemental kingdoms. Thus the responsiveness of these kingdoms to human attention and human implorations!

Men can be reached only through their True Selves, Who *is*

the Divine Father, the Source of All Principles and Thoughts and Things — Unity. Thus the power of Unity for those wise enough to exploit it in accordance with the Will for the All Highest Good.

WHAT IS OUR TRUE
CONDITION ON EARTH?

Man, in his present condition on Earth, can best be described as a hypnotized being. The term *asleep* was used by Gurdjieff to describe Man's state here, but that term is slightly inaccurate in that it is quite possible for a sleeping man to know that he is asleep — this recognition during dreams is fairly common for many members of our species — whereas almost never does a deeply hypnotized man ever realize that he is hypnotized. Man is hypnotized via his senses into believing that the body-consciousness is his *true* consciousness, and that all the things he sees, hears, tastes, and smells are real and not subservient to him and his will.

Nevertheless, *asleep* is still the preferred term for describing Man's earthly condition, because all people to whom this important thought is being conveyed will have known firsthand the experience called *sleep* whereas very few of you will have experienced hypnosis firsthand.

You know, for example, that in your sleeplife you sometimes dream and sometimes you "check out" of all activity to rest and drift dreamlessly. This is the way your earthlife is: periods of activity in "reality" alternating with periods of sleep.

You also know that in your dreams you quite often are unaware of who you are and where you are, and how you ended up in your current situation, and even maybe who some of your companions are, even though you seem to know them and they you. This is *exactly* akin to earthlife. You do not know who you really are — you think that you are some name your parents gave your physical body, or worse: that you *are* your physical body. You do not know what it is that got you chained to this beautiful planet called Earth, or what got you chained to your physical body, a body sadly subject to death and decay. And just as it never occurs to you to ask the answers to these questions in your dreams, so do so very few of you ever bother to ask in your earthlife.

Most of you have experienced an abrupt awakening from a bad dream just as you had fallen from a cliff, or were about to be shot at point-blank range, or to become a pariah or outcaste within your social group. And so it is with earthlife — a sudden awakening at the moment of physical death, an awakening into a realm of higher consciousness which makes a man realize finally that he had indeed been asleep all of those years, and that it was only a bad dream.

A great many of you can comfortably accept the highly rational concept of reincarnation, and can allow as how yes, Earth is a classroom, and sooner or later when we have mastered all the lessons it has to teach us, we shall graduate to a higher plane of existence or at least to a more perfect planet and physical body.

Well, it is not quite that easy. Look at the progress Man has made over the last few millenia — if anything he knows and understands even less of the Hermetic Wisdom than he did 6000 years ago — and he still kills off his fellows with monotonous regularity but on a vaster, more efficient scale.

Did you say that we have advanced in technology over those millenia? With all of our modern technology, we could not build a Great Pyramid. It matters not whether the Great Pyramid's technology had other-world origins or not, the fact is that our forebears of that era were made beneficiaries of that technology but, like us, their intrinsic worth as human beings is not changed one iota by technology except in one respect: if it frees them from time-consuming mundane labors and if they apply some of the saved time in acquiring knowledge of themselves — who they are, where they are, how they got where they are, and where if anywhere they are going. And what do we of the current age use the time saved by technology for? For TV, dances, pleasure shopping, water-skiing, pinball playing, daydreaming, getting drunk, or maybe just cruising Main Street. All human pastimes are used by us for one purpose: to help us forget that *we are going to die!* Instead of deciphering death and knowing its cause and overcoming it, we would rather just try to forget it and hope that perhaps it will go away.

It will not go away. Not in this lifetime, not in your last 450 lifetimes, and not in your next 450 lifetimes. It will not go away. Sooner or later, you are going to have to confront it, to investigate it in its truest light, and then by virtue of knowing what it is, to *conquer* it.

That is the only way you will ever escape this Malefic Illusion. You must conquer it by knowledge of yourself and ergo, by knowledge of death. This is one true instance where knowledge — or Wisdom — is indeed Power. Knowing who you are and what death really is will free you of your body of death and decay and restore you to a permanent body in what is commonly called Paradise, or Heaven. It is the only way free of death, and the only way off of Earth, albeit there may be many paths to the attainment of this knowledge, this realization.

If not now, eventually you will tire of the pain and heartache that accompany earthly existence, and of the misery caused by the ignorance which binds you to Earth, and you will set yourself free. So why not now? Why not save yourself a great deal of needless suffering? Why not *ask?*

IS THERE ANY TRUTH TO THE CONCEPT OF ORIGINAL SIN?

Perverted creature that I am, I have always been given, on seeing a decrepit and withered old lady, to imagine her as she must have been as a frisky five-year-old apple-of-her-daddy's-eye. I have always been dumbfounded that mere time can transform a frolicking, cheerful, tow-headed tot in sparkling white taffeta into a feeble, dour, and pain-stricken old lady.

And even more astonishing than this sad metamorphosis which is repeated endlessly for nearly every one of us who is born into this Vale of Tears, is the aplomb with which all men seem to accept this mockery of the Human Spirit. "It's natural," you will hear, from sage and fool alike, "birth, aging, death, are all part of nature's grand plan, and it is wise to accept them as they are and to yield gracefully to the inevitable." And few indeed are those who are stunned by the ludicrousness of the pristine and healthy youngsters slowly transforming themselves into the feeble, disease-ridden, cynical "senior citizens". A commendable few may feel compelled to resist or reverse the downhill ride to their involuntary exit from the corporeal form they inhabit, responding perhaps to a subconscious awareness that this is not necessarily the way things have to be. But where can such stalwart souls turn for sound advice and guidance? To cosmetic manufacturers and health-food promoters? To medical quacks hawking skin treatment schemes or wielding cosmetic surgery scalpels? To positive thinking advocates who assure us that old age is just an attitude, and disease a mere symptom of wrong thinking?

Of the lot, the last are closest to the Truth, but they do not tell the Whole Truth simply because they do not know It. The Whole Truth, which can set Man free of his earthly incumberance and free him of the grave of gravity, is harbored deep within the superconsciousness of most of us. It recurs over the millenia in myth and morality. It is the concept of original sin.

Men — even those without Puritan religious upbringing — know instinctively that the original sin is the sex act. Without any promptings or education whatsoever, male and female children of the earliest age will feel a sense of shame or naughtiness when they undertake to explore each other's bodies. They literally bring a knowledge of original sin into life with them, and any anthropologist or social scientest or psychologist

who will tell you otherwise is simply a person who has not properly investigated the matter.

And although Man collectively may not recall that the sex
act led to his fall from the "Garden of Eden", he collectively
suspects it because he has been told repeatedly, in times both ancient and modern. It is a message — a fact — which he most
assuredly does not want to hear, especially if he is new to the
species and has not had his fill of life as yet. Like any child who is
happily over-indulging himself with licorice candy, such men do
not want to think about the inevitable stomach ache that lies in
store for them when they pursue sex for pleasure.

And there are no large groups of earthly society anywhere,
now or in the past, which will not resist this Truth with all the
vehemence they can muster. For this is truly nature's way, and
not Man's — nature is impelled to keep Man enslaved to the
natural processes so that he can bring Light to the evolutionary
forces of nature's elements. By way of these elemental spirits,
and by way of their actions upon men who are enslaved to them,
no society will accept or tolerate for even a brief moment the idea
that the sex act is not in Man's best interests.

So if you tentatively accept this hypothesis and decide to
pursue it further to see where it may lead, do not expect much
company. Apparently in the past, singular seekers of Wisdom
and isolated small grouops of their followers may have accepted
the truth about the sex act, but where any small society of such
seekers was organized into being, they did, by virtue of their very
tenets, snuff themselves out of existence within a single generation. For very few, if any, of Man's earthly institutions can endure without the sex act.

Your beliefs and attitudes, if you should realize the enormous
import of this Truth, will immediately set you apart from your
fellow men, and in a manner not even remotely acceptable to
society. So you will, sad to say, need brace yourself against feelings of pariahship — of not being one of the crowd. These feelings
will become even more pronounced if the Truth "takes" with you,
and you begin to live a life of true celibacy. For as the changes in
attitudes and consciousness which this prctice brings begin to
take hold of you, you will find yourself strangely disassociated
and distant from the concerns of your fellow men. Things that are
important to almost all of our crowd begin to seem sheer folly to
you: politics, possessions, fashion, fame, social standing,
vaunting of the personal ego in any shape or form. And things

that are derided and scorned by almost all elements of society will become of paramount importance to you, even to the extent of becoming second nature to you: humility, unselfishness and a general dedication to the common good, a benign harmlessness even in self-defense, and most profound: a sense of growing detachment towards earthlife and its pleasures and pains and a mushrooming yearning to flee to a better place, a place where you sense you truly belong.

You may even someday find yourself transformed, like the Prophets of the Old Testament or the author of Ecclesiastes. For the earnest pursuit of Truth in Its highest form, not just for your own good but for the common good too, can indeed work miracles for you. And even if you just lift yourself, you have lifted all men, for such is the nature of the Most High Truth, *Unity*.

WHO ARE YOU?

The most amazing aspect about sleeping man is not that he is unaware of who or what he is, but that this unawareness troubles him not one whit. It is somewhat akin to a lost hiker who has fleeting moments of awareness that he may indeed be lost in the woods or desert, but never admits the fact to himself and — far worse — on encountering another being he will not only *not* ask where he is but will actually turn away from any such *volunteered* information!

It can be argued that if sleeping man is happy in his lost state it is therefore of no importance to him to rectify the situation. And this argument holds true from the short-term viewpoint. But eternity is not short-term, and eternity is all we have, so we must take the long-range viewpoint and admit that sooner or later the hiker must abandon his lost state or else encounter a great deal of needless — and like eternity, endless — suffering.

Those of you who do not mind needless suffering, and those of you who may even secretly crave it, have no need of this brief summary of *who you are*. The rest of you may want to pay attention.

To begin, you are an individual facet of the Eternal Father — a "soul", or ongoing personality manifestation — and you are also an awesome, towering, spiritual creation commonly called *Man*. If you do not understand how you can be both finite and infinite, you should ponder the nature of the hologram. You are a hologram of the Cosmos. You did not have a beginning, and you will not know an ending. Man is truly the Son of God, and yet is a God in his own right.

Because of this, your heritage, you constantly create a vivid reality, a veritable universe of realities, and then proceed to bask in your creation. The purpose is simple: for Holy Spirit to know Itself and what It is capable of. For existence and being, as opposed to dreamless sleep.

Man populates not only Earth but countless other physical universes as well. Man populates semi-physical realms such as the astral planes, and numerous spiritual or etheric realms wherein lie Man's more proper dwelling places.

Man can make mistakes, for a Creation without mistakes would also be a Creation without right action. Man can likewise be stupid or foolish because without these qualities, how could Intelligence and Wisdom be measured?

When Man becomes ensnared in a sleeping, dreamlike state such as you are in here on Earth, it is always attributable to stupidity and foolishness. How can a veritable God — Man — be stupid or foolish? For one reason only: to provide an avenue for his inherent intelligence and Wisdom to express themselves in the act of rescuing him.

And there in a nutshell you have an explanation of who you are. You may or may not come to understand it in the near future, but eventually you *will* come to understand it since it is your heritage to understand All Things, most especially your Self.

By the sheer force of your will, because you are who you are, you can create any condition of Reality which you may wish. But as the philosopher warned: take what you will, but be prepared to pay the price. So the first thing you should will — the very first thing above all others — is Wisdom. For when you have Wisdom, you can then proceed to will in harmony with All That Is and with All That You Are.

And your sleep, your ignorance, your suffering, may all come to an end.

WHERE DOES WISDOM COME FROM?

It is not an unreasonable question, when one is presented with the Eternal Wisdom, whether from discarnate or incarnate sources, to ask: where does Wisdom come from?

Well, if you want a physical analogy, it comes from within the heart of each of us as individuals, and from each of us as a collective group called Man, and from within the higher collective groups that we call Christ and the All Highest Father. For Man is a triune being, composed of the Father and the Son and the Holy Spirit, also often referred to as the Divine Mother, or Love — the concept of Form in whose womb dwell all things visible. She is Beauty Incarnate — Venus — the Virgin Mary and the Celestial Virgin, too. She is always portrayed as a virgin, the pinnacle of earthly concepts of purity. For She is indeed Pure in Her physical raiment, but Man's consciousness relentlessly violates Her purity. Man sees evil and harm in her allurements, but in actuality She cannot encompass such things. She is Purity! And only Man can defile Her by disavowing to look only at Her beauties and instead reveling in what to him appears dark and evil. For we men indeed do dwell in a state of lust, and to lust after any part of the Celedstial Virgin is to lust after Her Herself. To commit a negative comment about someone before friend or stranger is to do it before Her. To curse your luck or yourself or worse still, Creation, is for you to curse the Most Awesome Venus, the Intimate Mother of you, the Celestial Son. For to each of us she is a most intimate Mother. She is Mother Earth and Mother Nature.

Now Creation cannot exist without both a projection of Reality and a perception of Reality; we simply cannot have one without the other. They are the sides of a coin, male and female, the projector and the receptor. And we, being both male and female, have the ability to achieve an Immaculate Conception within ourselves, and to give birth to a higher Reality: the Son, the Living Christ, the Sun.

The Ever-Flaming One, the Son of Man, lies dormant as an unfertilized ovum within the heart of each of us. If we can balance the male and female aspects of ourselves, we can impregnate the ovum and eventually give birth to the Son of Man within us. We can achieve the Christ Consciousness, the Cosmic Consciousness, while still in flesh. In fact, as it ironically turns out, it is actually possible for Man, having fallen to Earth and having been chained to Earth, to make faster progress towards his reunion with the

Deity while in earthly flesh than it would have been had he pro-
gressed on his normal path. So his fall from grace actually works
to Man's advantage, placing him in such a focal point within
Creation, exactly midway at the critical junction of the
downward evolutionary path towards nature and the upward
evolutionary path towards Unity. But Man did not *evolve* to his
present lowly position in the Universe, he *fell*. For Man is a God,
toying with the concept of mortality. What does it matter how
long he tarries on Earth? He can step back to his true estate on a
moment's notice. He has all eternity in which to return to the
Father, so what do another fifty lifetimes cost if he is having
"fun" and truly enjoying the suffering that death and decay
bring?

But there is always that select group on Earth who have
grown tired of it, who yearn for something better — something
more permanent with no bad vibrations, free of deceit and
callousness and sophistication and jaded viewpoints, free of
cynical jibes, and of people who go unloved, and of people who are
so lost that they are not even aware of being lost.

There are always those who yearn for a Pure place, a place of
Infinite Beauty, a place of Truth and Wisdom. They are tired of
the earthly illusions, and they yearn to go home.

So to those yearners who ask, I say Wisdom does not come
from anywhere: it is All That Is, and Was, and Ever Will Be. For
Wisdom is Truth: Unity. Wisdom is the Eternal Truth of all matters and manifestations, the proper working out of the Infinite
Will.

Since Wisdom is everywhere, all one need do is to request it
and it is delivered. It is usually delivered through messengers
called "sages", much as Beauty is delivered by messengers called
Artists. Neither sage nor Artist creates anything that has not
always existed. They merely tap the Eternal Founts of these two
virtues called Wisdom and Beauty and deliver to us whatever
they happen to find there. If what they return with strikes a sympathetic response with the masses, they may become rich and
famous. If what they return with is too refined or premature, they
remain poor and obscure.

But true wise men, like true Artists, do not enter the
messenger business because they long to be rich or famous. They
live for that which they discover, and for the joy of sharing it
with their fellow man. They truly worship Beauty or Wisdom, or
both.

And so it is that the most profound Art radiates Wisdom, just as the most profound Wisdom radiates Beauty. The more these virtues seem to merge, the higher their individual expressions.

And this is why you should seek to balance the male and female within you: they are, respectively, your Wisdom and your Beauty. And more important, they are the paths to further Wisdom and Beauty.

You can discover firsthand, for example, that you have the power to shape your Reality in any way you see fit. In fact, this is what you constantly are doing, even now as you read these very words. You are literally manufacturing your Reality now and for the future. You are doing it by Thought. So if you do not like your present Reality, you have only yourself and your thoughts to blame.

If you seek Wisdom and Beauty, you will find them. You will find them in the Infinite Will, the Will for the All Highest Good. For it is willed that you shall seek Wisdom and Beauty. You shall know the flawless, unmarred, divinely Pure Beauty of All Creation. You shall return to your homeland.

These things are all destined to come to pass for you. The only thing left to your device and free will is to determine *when*.

WHY EVEN BOTHER
SEEKING WISDOM?

Most certainly the average man on the street might ask this question. And quite probably even a goodly percentage of you who have read thus far might throw up your hands and ask such a question. For most assuredly what you have read — and what you are going to read, should you continue — is not exactly what you want to hear.

The question is an understandable and forgivable one when things are going well for you in your earthly affairs. You may like your station in life and be succeeding at it, the kids are happy and healthy, your marriage is sound, and the little day-to-day pleasures such as food and sex and sleep and social contact all seem to combine to "make life worth living".

The only hitch is that what you so flippantly call "life" is not Life. From almost any observation point throughout the Cosmos, you are a member of the living dead — being held prisoner in a vast, outdoor madhouse. And like many asylum inmates who delude themselves into believing that they are *not* in an asylum and that wherever they are they are most assuredly there of their own volition, you are quite happy with your lot until the shock treatments and pre-frontal lobotomies begin.

You just might harbor a hint of your true situation the next time you say farewell to the remains of a loved one. Or when you send one of your progeny off to war, never to return. Or when those whom you most loved and trusted turn out to have only been jesting with your affections and faith. Or when you yourself lie wasting away in pain, with tubes and wires and needles sprouting like obscene spaghetti from your physical frame. Or when you give up hope in yourself and humanity for sundry reasons and walk the streets alone, knowing that no one in the whole mad world really cares whether you live or die or rehabilitate.

A morbid and unfair view of our estate, you may be thinking. Life, after all, is not really that bad unless you make it so. And therein lies the rub! This indeed is what we, individually and collectively, are making of "life". We are doing it to ourselves! The pain, the sorrow, the death and decay are all of our own making! And it is all for the lack of Wisdom.

But an opportunity for many of us to step out of this mould is dawning. It is an opportunity born of our solar system's sojourn through the Cosmic Womb. It is most commonly called the "Age of Enlightenment" or the "New Age" by those harbingers, both mortal and non-mortal, who recognize and proclaim it. It is our choice to listen to them, and hopefully to hear what they are saying, or to continue on our merry way towards another lengthy tenure in the asylum. We can number ourselves among the chosen, wherein it is really we who are doing the choosing, or we can go on being nature's fodder for another seemingly endless round of birth, decay, and death.

It is of paramount importance to you first to realize that you have a choice — not just now but always — to awaken from this mad dream, and second to accept the fact that what is apparently about to befall Earth and its minions is a golden opportunity for you to break with consumate ease the ties that bind!

The essential realization for you to attain is, above all, that you are God and that you have complete control over your destiny at all times. The next most essential realization is one that you already have, and that just manifested itself as you read the preceding sentence: that you are asleep and do not know your true Self or your true powers, and that therefore it is not going to be easy to break out of the trap. And so we come to the third and most important realization in the current time frame: that there is such a thing as *Grace*, and that your being where you are today is an overpowering example of Grace.

Because even if you are not among the chosen, having not yet chosen yourself so to be, you are indeed among the select. You would not be reading these words if you were not. You are among the select few within history for whom graduation from this sphere of insanity can be effected with minimum risk and effort. You can escape the need for lengthy purification that ordinarily is prerequisite to the immaculate conception of your True Self. You can bypass the agony of the Cross. Because of the age upon which we on Earth now embark, you can, colloquially, be privy to taking the easy way out.

And this in the final analysis can for us be the highest Wisdom of all — to know a golden opportunity when we see it and to capitalize on it with confidence, with joy, and above all, with *gratitude*.

YOU, AND YOU ALONE

There are no wise men, there are only those men who are adept conduits for waters from the Eternal Fount of Wisdom. Having slaked your thirsts before, hold out your cups and let us fill them anew with what we have collectively channelled from that Sacred Pool.

Wisdom cannot exist, save that it be recognized. Just as a tree falling in a forest makes no noise if there are no ears to hear it, so can the Concept of Wisdom have no existence unless there be those who recognize It and love It. And neither can any single element of Wisdom have validity except that there be a mind somewhere to savor it.

Thus you are a valid co-creator of all that you treasure, which is of course your Reality and all of those "separate" events and things which go to make it up. If you love a symphony or film, you are co-creator of that symphony or film. If you love another human personality, you are co-creator of that human personality, for it would adjust itself accordingly if it did not meet with your loving approval.

All which you perceive of the nature kingdom, and which constitutes "life" for you, is co-created by you. In Man's Reality, there can be no projection without perception. For such to be possible would also allow for the possibility of the one-ended stick: some things cannot be! You co-create all things which are real to you, and so you are a creator of Wisdom and Beauty and Truth if these Ideals be real to you.

Now pause for a moment and look at a tree. Ask yourself: where did the Idea of trees come from? Where did the Idea of that particular tree emanate? No matter what answers you give yourself to these questions, you will find with but a few moments' conjecturing that both Ideas are intimately connected with one another. They are, in fact, hopelessly entangled. The Idea of that particular tree you are looking at is part of the Idea of trees in general, and vice versa. And further it is also part of the Idea of that building in front of which or inside of which the tree may be standing, and it is part of every Idea which that building is connected with, and it is *even part of that Idea of you looking at the tree to ponder its identity*! It is therefore a most intimate part of the Idea that is manifesting as you! In other words, that individual tree, as an Idea, is as hopelessly entangled with all other Ideas in Creation as it is with the Idea of trees in general.

That tree is the Stuff of Consciousness Itself. If you can perceive the Beauty of its Reality — in its physical form, in its mental, or Idea, form, and in its spiritual or Love form — then so much the better. But all you need perceive for the purposes of our current discussion is the mental Idea form of that single tree itself, and you will find that it is naught but Consciousness: Creative Consciousness conceiving of the Idea, and your use of that same Conscious Stuff to *perceive* the Idea. Together this male/female, yin/yang operation is what we men recognize as Creation — All That Is — the Trinity of Father, Son, and Mother. It is all nothing but Consciousness in Its three aspects of operation: projection, perception, and Reality. The perfect synonym for Reality, which is the Mother in Her form as the Celestial Virgin or Mother Nature or however you may care to worship Her, is *Love*. For this is what Reality truly is, and this is what Love truly is in its purest, most absolute, most holy manifestation. And no mattter which of these three functions is being performed by Consciousness — projection, perception, Love — the performance utilizes the Stuff of Consciousness, the only construction material that exists anywhere in the Cosmos.

That particular tree which you observe is Reality, and is thereby conscious of its being a tree, but it is Reality only because you as perceptor and the *Real You* as projector have made it Reality. So love it! Love it as you would your own progeny, for verily it stems from within your heart of hearts. There lie its mental roots and its spiritual roots, whereas Mother Earth has custody only of its physical roots.

It and you are more related than you can ever consciously appreciate, so you must use your mystical consciousness to fully be aware of your intimate kinship with that tree and with *everything else you see or are made aware of*! You and the tree and All Things are truly One! You are fashioned from one Store of Consciousness, and that Consciousness is *you* in all of your manifestations: as a human or an insect or a plant or a mountain or a galaxy.

If you perceive even an inkling of Wisdom in these observations, you cannot help but love All Things as yourself, including your neighbor. For they, and he, and she, and *It*...they *are* yourself.

WHY YOU MUST HELP HEAL EARTH

Earth is a devoted Mother — so devoted that she will not even release us from her womb. Every morsel we eat, the air we breathe, and the liquids we drink, come from Mother Earth. You may think you are eating cow or pig, but that cow and that pig built their flesh from atoms sent up by Mother Earth in the form of plants.

Every atom of your physical being has come from Mother Earth in the form of gases and minerals and plants. As a physical outcropping of our planet, the only difference between you and a tree is that you are mobile and not tied to one spot on Earth.

You quite naturally feel a close bond with your birth mother. After all, she carried you for nine months and formed your original body from particles of her own physical body. Her blood was your blood, her oxygen your oxygen, her nutrients your nutrients. The two of you where one human organism for the first nine months of your life, a strange and miraculous human organism with two heartbeats and *two hearts*! Add to this the fact that she probably nurtured you so closely during your formative years outside her womb and you have the basis for the strongest bond possible among earthly men: mother and child.

Even in those instances where a mother dislikes her children and maybe even abandons them, the mother-child tie is still perhaps the strongest bond that either of them will ever know during their lives. And here is where women indeed have the advantage over men: they can experience both ends of this unique bond during their lifetimes!

Yet as close as you may feel to your birth mother, you are going to have to admit to a far closer relationship with your Earth Mother. The reasons you must admit this are as follows: (1) While your birth mother was carrying you in her womb, your Earth Mother was carrying the *both* of you in Her womb, for were you or your mother or any human being to leave the Earth Womb, you would encounter certain physical death. (2) You and Mother Earth comprise a single organism at all times throughout your life, whereas you and your birth mother were so joined for a paltry nine months. (3) If you feel some sort of bond with your ancestors or other "blood" relatives, be aware that your Earth Mother was a most intimate and sustaining mother to each and every one of them, on both sides of your family tree, for as far back and as far sideways as you care to measure. (4) And the most important reason of all is this: that being thus so intimately bound physically, it is inevitable that there would also be a spiritual bond between you and Earth. And there is indeed! The Earth is a Most High Spiritual Entity, in Whom rest the souls and psyches of billions of Its children over the past eons, including you. Some have graduated onto higher planes and are thus free of Earth's sphere of influence, but they left with respect for a Most High Being, a Planetary Logos, and his consort on the planes of form, Mother Earth. The Spirit of the Logos impregnated Earth Ether and gave birth to you, the Son, in a sparkling conception. The physical counterpart to that act of spiritual intercourse is sexual intercourse, and both are capable of producing living independent beings out of seed and pattern and Light. The seed of the Planetary Logos is Love — Spirit going out to know Itself. The seed of man may spring from pure lust, but it too, in and of itself, is Love, an embodiment of purest Light. The concepts of sperm and ova, of cells and DNA, combining to reproduce the most complex of living physical organisms, is Love at one of Its highest creative levels. The concept of the sex act and its powerful hold on mortal humans is likewise a brilliant bit of creation.

Now having had to admit to closer bonds to your Earth Mother than to your birth mother, you have an answer to the question: why you must help heal Earth. To heal her is to heal yourself; to heal yourself is to heal her. Indeed, the only reason she needs healing at all is because we, her human offspring, have injured here and sickened her through our corrupt behavior.

What birth mother would not be made heartsick even unto death if her children were to go about slaying each other out of greed and intolerance? What birth mother does not suffer in her heart over the sufferings of her offspring? And how much more hurtful would her suffering be if her childrens' suffering were caused by her other children?

How much pain does Earth feel not only when we go about untouched by her beauty, but when we through callousness or greed pollute or destroy that beauty? How much of Mother Earth's aura is torn or dirtied by our violently negative thoughts and acts? What agony do we cause her when we hurl daggars of hate at a sibling? What heartbreak does she endure when we turn away coldly from a needy one — the exact equivalent of turning her away in her most desperate need since she and the downtrodden are one even as she and you are one?

We have wounded Mother Earth almost beyond repair. She is ready to abandon her association with human life on the physical plane, and the coming polar shift with its prospects for the total elimination of human life does not disturb her. In our present stage of development, the less human life she nurtures, the less suffering she must endure. She is *weary*, I tell you: *weary* from our lack of progress and the spiraling Karmic debt we are accruing. She is depleted from mothering the most morally backward "civilization" in the Cosmos.

To save her, you have to help heal her. And this you do by healing yourself. Purify your thoughts, and thereby your acts. Think with probity and you shall act with probity. Then cleanse your emotions. Take the most sacred vow you can conceive of to not be a channel for any more negative energy. Pledge to immediately identify anger, resentment, jealousy, or enmity when they first approach you, and to turn them aside at once. Pray to the All Highest Father that your consciousness be prodded awake the second it yields to these emotions, or to hopelessness or fear, or to brooding anxious feelings about non-existent future disasters. And when you thus are jolted into an awareness of what you are thinking and of its negative nature, remember your vow and terminate the thought immediately.

You will have the power to do this if you have the will. You can demonstrate your good will right now, by taking the vow. It is preferable to take the vow verbally. If you have to write the vow first before you can verbally utter it, so much the better. Take an oath to, and in the name of, all those beings you hold most sacred. And by all means include the Highest Being of All, the All Highest Father.

It may just turn out that only the pure in heart will be saved for the continuing population of Mother Earth after Armageddon. You can qualify for this mission if you so wish by healing yourself, purifying yourself, and thus helping in the healing of Mother Earth. But even if you are to be among the "saved" who leave Earth for their natural kingdom, you can enhance your qualifications for that mission also — merely by healing yourself and thus helping to heal Mother Earth.

Who among you would not do this for your birth mother? Who among you would not assuage the sorrows of the Celestial Virgin? Who among you is so blind that you cannot see the Truth of what you have just read?

WHY IT IS IMPORTANT TO ALIGN YOUR WILL WITH THE WILL OF THE ALL HIGHEST FATHER

It is because no creature — animate or inanimate, organic or non-organic — on any plane of existence *ever suffers* when the Will of The All Highest Father is being brought to pass. So it stands to reason that you, a creature, would not then suffer if the Will of The All Highest God were to be made manifest in your life.

So if for no other reason than as a surefire tool for avoiding suffering, you should adopt the Divine Will as your will. Your new Reality — the Reality that you co-create with the Divine Spirit that projected the world — will supplant the old reality, created in the same manner, except the new creation will be from an unselfish focus. You, the Divine Spirit who sees the world, will co-create this greater Reality with your Better Half — your most true Bride or Bridegroom — with whom you can unite in giving birth to the Son of Awareness, the Immaculate Conception which underwrites the myth of the events surrounding Jesus of Nazareth's birth.

Conceive of your Better Half in whatever form you may care to, but always be reminded of the fact that your Better Half is a spiritual being. It is pure. And it is your most highly-conceivable complement. It is the Self for which you constantly yearn, and which by its seeming absence drives you to the constant seeking of distractions, and to alcohol or drugs, and to idle pursuits of personal desires — usually desires for sensual gratification — and to self-punishment in every shape and form via the sowing of bad Karma. By not recognizing the Divine Spirit within you, you are driven to bring harm to other creatures, and thus you bring a terrible Reality to bear on yourself, for to harm anything or anyone in Creation is to harm yourself in that your are One with All That Is.

The way to unite with this Better Half of you, and to bring the Will of the All Highest Father to pass, is to blend your will with the All Highest Will and to give birth to the Son of Reason, the Sun of Light, the Omnipresent, Omniscient, and Omnipotent One, the Living Christ, your personal Lord *no matter what your religious faith may authorize.* This is the secret of the power of Christianity — it not only preaches the Wisdom of the Ages, the One God, Unity — but it preaches also the highly mystical and true fact of the Trinity — the triune nature of Man's being. And above all, on the seventh level of understanding, it preaches the extremely occult truth of Man's surest salvation from death, decay, and suffering — the Immaculate Conception. By allegory, the Life of Jesus was a highly mystical passion play, one which even today continues to work itself out in its nuances, intents, and historic realities. There is no question as to its Reality — it is the Essence of Reality, for men have lived it properly ever since the events came into being. Men — not many, but also not few — have been sacrificing their personal wills, their small selves, on the Cross of Time and Space; and by losing their lives they have gained Life — the Reality of the All Highest Good.

The Living Christ transcends time and space and yet is a part of them via His existence in you. He is the fiery core of your being: your physical being, your mental being, and your spiritual being. He is the Unity of your Triune Self. He is the Eternal One. He is your next-door neighbor, the paper boy, and your mother and father. He is the violet sunrise of the mountains, the spring green of their Mayday aspens, the pure white snow on their craggy peaks. He is all of your senses and all of your experiences. He is closer than hands and feet, nearer than breathing. The two of you are never apart, except within your own sleep-deadened mind and the false reality it produces.

The spirit that sleeps creates an illusory world of separation — a world of death, decay, and pain. The awakened spirit most likely awakened itself by aligning and dedicating its will to the Will of the All Highest Good, and so it quite naturally creates an ideal world, the world of truest Reality, the world willed into being by the Creative Spirit Itself: the World of Unity!

THE NEUTRALIZING FORCE

Gurdjieff somehow knew the importance of the Neutralizing Force. And all men of scientific wisdom know the importance of this Force, particularly in its manifestation in the form of the neutrino.

Men of all persuasions — philosophical, mystical, or scientific — are aware of the pervasiveness and importance of the male/female principles. The positive/negative, projection/perception aspects of Absolute Reality are reflected in every layer of physical reality, mental reality, and spiritual reality.

But in the individual personality manifestations throughout the Omniverse, it is usually considered to be poor form to allow one or the other of the male/female aspects to dominate. It is not a mortal sin or even a venial sin to do so: just poor form. But to the victims of this imbalance it may indeed seem like a sin due to the suffering it brings about. Decay and death, and the concepts fostering these phenomena, are activated through the imbalance of the male/female principles when the imbalance is wilfully adopted by a spiritual being. And since Man is a spiritual being, he has concocted myths about mortal sin and original sin. The only sin is ignorance, so it would be better to term the basic problem Man has with death and decay as an outgrowth of original ignorance, rather than of original sin.

The more evolved a creature stands in the Cosmos, the more likely it is to be sexless, or more accurately, androgynous. *Sexless* implies an absence of the male/female forces; *androgynous* implies an abundance of these forces, but in a balanced state, a neutralized state. Angels manifest this condition almost always, and they indeed are highly evolved beings.

The visitors from other worlds who are well documented in the UFO literature appear to be more highly evolved than we are — more evolved scientifically at least and most apparently morally also. They eschew warfare and the killing and maiming of their own or other species, and they soundly condemn this practice by Man. These visitors almost always, but not always, manifest as androgynous: either of an indeterminate sex, or all apparently of the same "sex". And those who manifest otherwise may indeed be only masquerading as male or female to render themselves and therefore their messages more comprehensible or more palatable to Man.

And so important questions begin to arise for those people

who can spot a trend and who then decide that they just might have a chance to get out of the male/female death/decay loop. What brings about the balancing of the male/female forces? Is it itself a force? How does one invoke it? What in fact *is* it?

Well, it IS the ultimate IS. It IS the Father of All Creation. It IS both a balancing force and a unifying force; It IS that beyond all manifestation. It IS the primordial Consciousness which both projects and perceives All That Is in the Cosmos, and which renders tender Truth to the awesome reality and majesty of Existence. It IS the creator of both male and female forces, and these forces were Its first creations. It IS the only force which can neutralize and balance the male/female forces. It IS Unity, the All Highest Father: Creation.

By seeking to lose yourself to this Force, you begin to neutralize the male/female impolarities which may exist at any level of your being. As your personality expands to embrace the All Highest, you actually appear to those around you to be *diminishing* in personality, because you are no longer solely Earth-centered, whereas they are.

And eventually you will become an androgynous being, immune to death/decay, and capable of transcending the mortal coil at will. You will be more male than the most macho redneck street-fighter, and you will be more female than any Hollywood sex queen could possibly show herself to be. But you will be balanced, and you will be Whole, for you will have regained your lost Estate through the Neutralizing Force.

INVOKING THE
NEUTRALIZING FORCE

God-consciousness on a daily basis will invoke the Neutraliz-ing Force. By the term "God-consciousness" it is meant that you expand your consciousness outward towards the shell of the Cosmic Egg, seeking to embrace with love and understanding All That Is, and that you also expand your consciousness inward towards the center of the Cosmic Egg, seeking to embrace your True Source with love and understanding.

Within you, located physically near your heart, is a spark of the Divine Father, your personal inlet to God, to All That Is. This spark can be turned into a flame by way of your attentiveness to it. This flame can, in and of itself, transform you without the need for any other act or thought for assistance.

You help fan this flame not only by attentiveness to it, but also by expanding outward to see that All That Is is not only everywhere but is also in reality an integral part of you. You iden-tify with Unity, with Creation, and you identify yourself as both the Creator and the Observer of all that you think and see and taste and feel. You identify therefore with the Neutralizing Force, the Force which stands above both male/female forces and projec-tion/perception forces.

The Neutralizing Force balances your male/female forces by absorbing them within Itself. It also strengthens and enhances the male/female forces as It absorbs them. When all three are perfectly harmonized with each other, you have a triangle: thus the mysteries of Pythagoras.

But in reality you have more of a pyramid — four triangles — since earthbound man is a fourfold being in his purely physical constitution. Thus you have the mysteries of the Ancient Egyp-tians and of all those who shared their knowledge so generously with the Ancient Egyptians.

WHO IS CHRIST?

When most men refer to Christ, they are knowingly or unknowingly referring to the Inner Self of all men. This is termed, quite properly, the Christ Self. It is the Living Presence, " closer than hands and feet and nearer than breathing". It is your True Self. It is Unity — the Alpha and Omega — Purest Consciousness — All That Is. You cannot permanently shut yourself off from It. It and you are One. It and all things and all beings are One.

If you would manifest your Christ Self, you can do no worse than follow the behavior pattern and philosophy and teaching of Jesus of Nazareth. He manifested the Christ Spirit in a sevenfold manner, appealing to men at every possible level of their development, and speaking to them in their language be it symbolic or earthly or mystical.

But there are and have been other notable exponents of the Divine Will, and there always will be others, for it is the Divine Will that man should know Who and What It is, as well as that Man should be convinced beyond a reasonable doubt that It exists. The Divine Will is the essence of All things, the Living Christ, the Incarnation of Love. It embraces the All Highest Good.

The uniting of your will with the Divine Will is the most sacred mission a human being can undertake. It is the Divine commitment. Baptism is the Christian symbolic act for this Commitment, but baptism can occur before or after the Commitment, or not at all, and still the Commitment can be successfully and sacredly made.

It is not possible for true harm to befall you once you have made this Commitment. It is the surest path to peace of mind, salvation, and unfoldment that a human being can take.

Uniting your will with the Divine Will involves: (1) listening to the Inner Voice when confronted with a decision or a need to judge the truth or falsity of a situation or issue; (2) giving thanks for all things; and (3) asking daily, in the name of Christ, that the Father make His Will manifest through you.

The requirements are so simple and so easily fulfilled that it is a wonder that all of us do not meet them.

THE MYSTERY OF CHRIST

And so we have explained to us in earthly language the Mystery of Christ. Because the mystery is so awesome, the earthly explanation is highly inadequate, but it is still better than no explanation at all.

The Christ Spirit is the unifying Spirit, and it is the recognition and exploitation of that Spirit which yields the Voice of Wisdom. It is the Voice which Jesus of Nazareth used most frequently during the last three years of his servitude to the men of Earth.

This Voice sings the same Divine Refrain over and over again, through endless eons. It is also the Voice of Creation, the Voice of Love, and foremost the Voice of the most tender compassion. It is Compassion Incarnate, for It is the Voice of That which embraces All That Is, and you cannot be anything *but* compassionate, loving, and forgiving towards that which is an integral part of you.

This Voice is the Voice of the Eternal Father. It is the Voice of the Celestial Virgin, the Divine Mother of Form and Spirit. And It is the Voice of the Prodigal Son who awakens to his heritage in a manner best exemplified by the life of Jesus and his teachings, and by the mystical myths which later grew from his life and techings.

No one man can fathom this Mystery, and yet each one of us embodies it. We plumb its depths only when we unite collectively in a spirit of true self-sacrifice. We gain our lives only when we sacrifice them. We progress only through service to Unity.

Each one of us is a channel for the Voice. Nothing new can come from the Voice via any mechanism — no new Truths, no new Wisdom — for All That Is is All That Ever Was and All That Ever Will Be.

No religious creeds or cults can stand against this fact, no matter what form their tenets or dogma may take, for this is Ultimate Truth, this Truth called Unity. It is the Highest Wisdom, and if one would ask of the Eternal Father, the Infinite Creator, what commandment one must follow first, last, and always, it is this: obey this single Truth, practice to the fullest your awareness of this Truth, and give voice to the undying Wisdom of the Ages.

WHAT IS THE TRUTH
ABOUT JESUS OF NAZARETH?

Whether or not you were born a Christian, and whether or not you believe the Christian dogma if you were born or converted to that religion, you are a manifestation of the Christ Spirit, for It is your True Self. Christ is that common Self of men, angels, minerals, and vegetables. He is the Eternal Father, and the Son of Man. He is Man struggling to find his True Self, and He is that True Self.

The Creative Force unites with the Divine Virgin, the Eternal Mother, and voila! you have Creation. And you have *you*, the Eternal Son. But only when you know who you are, who you *really* are, are you a Christed Being: aware of your oneness with All That Is.

Many men have walked the Earth who were Christed Beings, and who therefore manifested the Christic Peace, the Christic Benevolence, and the Christic Wisdom. Christians who follow the faith rever Jesus of Nazareth for the Christic Wisdom which he manifested as a Christed Being. This Wisdom enabled Jesus of Nazareth to perform feats which to the unwise appeared to be miracles. But Jesus of Nazareth was none other than a devout and holy seeker of Wisdom who, by prearrangement before his physical birth, was led to the greatest gurus of the Himalayas and to the wisest and most circumspect of the Mystery Schools, and eventually to the Great Pyramid at Gizeh, wherein he attained the final initiation and became a Christed One: an embodiment of the Spirit of Unity and Truth and flawless, untainted, undying Love for each and every one of His beings, no matter how humble, how broken, how evil, how despised of men, no matter how they may even spit at the mention of His name. He bore and he bears the most tender Love that one being can bear for another — the Love that a being feels for itself, a Love that your True Self feels for you when you think of It and yearn to know It, and to be one with It by submitting your small self and its ineffectual, misguided will to It and Its Will.

What Jesus was, was a highly concentrated focus of The Christ, our Common Self, for the purpose of enlightening Man for all time, and for the purpose of effecting certain magnetic adjustments to the Earth's lower three planes. The Christ has manifested with such brilliance before, even in men unknown to history, for it was not always essential to enact the Passion Play and thus achieve lasting fame as a standard bearer for the Christ Spirit as did Jesus of Nazareth.

The amazing thing is that the Christ Spirit is constantly manifesting in all of us — again, even within those who would spit at the mention of the name *Christ*. And the higher personality essence of Christ can speak briefly through any one of us at any time, for He has no limitations and can and does observe all that we see and do and think. When most in need of sound advice or enlightenment, He will sense your need and often address you through another being — a stranger or friend or brother or mother, it matters not — and He will even hold a lengthy conversation with you through that being. Or He may, as your True Self, gain temporary control over your petty, illusory self, and lead you to a place or book wherein His words are enscribed.

And He will most surely do all of these things almost constantly if you manifest Peace and Benevolence for All Things. He will also do these things if you seek to know Him, or if you seek intercession with Him through the Divine Mother in the highest form of which you can conceive of Her, or if you seek Wisdom, Beauty, or Truth in any of their forms.

You can also manifest Oneness with Him by sacrificing your petty self, by subordinating your small self and its pitiful will to your Higher Self and the Will of the All Highest Good. You see, there are always many paths to God. A Christed guru can always take you to your True Self via the Mystery School and initiation route. You can even get there by the opposite path, the lefthand path of consummate, unredeemable evil, whereby you are reducted into the Cosmic Mind through the route you exited, and it becomes as though you had never even existed as a separate entity.

The normal paths allow the evolving entity — who is really naught but God in a restricted form — to expand and to contain the Christed Self within it, an unflowering and semenization as it were, a mating of the opposing male and female forces within the being to produce the Immaculate Conception and to lead to the birth of the Son of Man within you, a mere mortal.

So Jesus of Nazareth deserves your respect and gratitude for his service to Man, but your worship: *never*! He himself would make this known to all men. Worship is reserved for The Christ, the Unifying Spirit, the Essence of Unity: my True Self, Jesus of Nazareth's True Self, and your True Self.

THE TRUTH ABOUT WEALTH

The definitive Wisdom on wealth, meaning wealth of mammon, is that the truth can be whichever way you want it to be: wealth is bad for you, or it is harmless to you. These two choices, however, are the only ones. The third option, that wealth is *good* for you, is not a possible one since it simply is not true.

And yet, oddly enough, wealth can indeed be good for those men to whom it comes as a result of their knowing the Truth that Man is God and can thus take anything that he so chooses — anything at all. And if richness of mammon excites Man, there is no earthly reason why he should not embrace it so long as he believes or knows that there is no harm in prosperity. Man can have it for the asking. But as always, he has to remember the adage: "Take what thou wilt, o Man, but be prepared to pay the price".

That phrase was addressed to those men who obtain wealth by stealth, by outwitting their fellow men, or by stealing, murder, the promotion of petty vices, or by any other act directed against a human being or humankind in general. But a man who gains wealth honorably, such as by the profession of a rare skill in show business or sports or art, or by the addition of or the augmenting of a work of beauty or wisdom, or by ministering unselfishly to humans in medicine or the social services, or by being a loyal servant who always holds his patrons' best interests at heart, or by writing or producing entertainments for the public, or by promoting Earth's bounties through farming or mining, or by inventing an ingenious device, or by sheeer stature of fame for some notable achievement of the human spirit — you who attain wealth in these fashions or by inheritance or blind luck — can rest assured that your wealth shall do you no harm.

You who get rich otherwise had best "sell all that you have and give it to the poor". You had best effect an immediate redistribution of your wealth, for your own sake only and not for the sake of others. For you know deep inside that you have taken what was not rightfully yours. Your True Self knows this. And your True Self, your Lasting Self — your *soul* if you will — is One within you and is One with all other beings, including those whom you cheated or robbed. And so to hurt them or to take from them is to hurt or take from yourself, and you will — for the Law so states it — you *will* pay back every cent you took unfairly. There simply is no escaping it.

The Law of Karma is the most important law of which mortals can be aware, for the mortal mind takes an extremely foreshortened view of Eternity. To most people, Eternity is the 70 or so years they live on Earth and anything before or beyond that is hogwash. They are totally out of touch with their Eternal Selves, which is also the Eternal Self of us all. If they can accept that the Law of Karma *is*, and that its impersonal mode of operation is similar to the law of gravity, they could save themselves much needless suffering.

So yes, wealth is bad for a man if he obtains it dishonorably. Otherwise, it is bad for a man only if he *believes* it to be bad for him, and especially if he therefore bears a burden of guilt for his possessions. If he be one of these, he should assure himself of two Eternal Truths: that no purpose whatsoever would be served among the poor if he were to join their ranks, and that he who has wealth is much better positioned to promote the pursuit of Wisdom and the dissemination of Beauty. He who has wealth has not only the wherewithal for these endeavors, but also has the luxury of time which these pursuits usually require in great doses.

So there should never be a feeling of guilt accompanying honorably-obtained wealth. Wealthy people do indeed have a duty to share some of their wealth with the less fortunate, but by no means need they give up all or even a major portion of their wealth.

So to those of you who are not yet wealthy but would like to be, all you need do is take it. If you do not become wealthy, it is for one of two reasons: you believe it to be immoral or unspiritual to be wealthy, or you secretly believe that you do not deserve to be wealthy.

But the Truth is this: so long as there is but one human anywhere on this planet who is travelling first class, you have an equal right to such treatment. The jetsetters are no better or more deserving than you. So long as there is one person driving the kind of car that you would most like to drive, it serves no good purpose for you to refuse to join his ranks on some pretense of not being worthy of such satisfaction, or that driving such cars is somehow evil.

All of you who desire — truly desire — to be wealthy, can be. Just *take*! *Take* wealth! The Cosmos is a bountiful cornucopia! It will overflow your life with blessings if you just *take* them. *Accept* them. There is absolutely nothing wrong with so doing.

And if so be it that wealth of mammon is not your heart's desire — if so be it that wealth of Wisdom or wealth of Consciousness be your most fervent desire — then *take* that wealth too, instead of the superficial wealth. You may find it infinitely more satisfying.

Wealth is there for the asking!

IS IT WRONG TO EXPLOIT FOR GAIN A MOST VITAL UNIVERSAL LAW?

There is a very potent Law, or Principality of Concept, in the Universe which can make anyone who exploits it a worldly wealthy individual. It is understandable that having been advised earlier to *take wealth* from the great cornucopia of the Cosmos, that you would now be wondering "How do I go about *taking* it? Do I take it from my neighbor? From the local bank? From what do you actually *take wealth*?"

The answer to this question is contained in this tract, as follows.

You do not take wealth from any one entity, you take it from the Cosmos. And you take it by exploiting a startling but consistent, and eminently vital Universal Principle: *you give!*

No one can truly understand why this Principle should apply with such consistency, but it does. It is almost a physical fact of the Universe that the more you give, the more is returned to you. You literally cannot deplete your holdings — the Cosmos will not permit it! So it is probably no accident that there are so many wealthy philanthropists in our world. They suspect the truth of this Law. They have always given heartily to worthwhile causes, which act has helped make them rich, and so they sentimentally or superstitiously continue such giving even after they have acquired all the money they will ever need.

Of course, they had to take some action on their own — to apply some of their own elbow grease. But in so doing, they found that they had phenomenal good luck. They made incredibly astute investments, engineered ingenious and well-timed business maneuvers, or just plain fell into a fortune through what their compatriots would acknowledge to be *pure luck*. In all these instances, however, *pure luck* is the key. The Cosmos paid them back with interest for that which they gave to others.

Now having been told of this Law, you may therefore be faced with the same moral dilemma that I was faced with, a dilemma that leads to the title of and the need for this particular tract. Knowing the Law of Giving and its unwaveringly consistent workings, would it not therefore be wrong to exploit it for the sake of enhancing one's own personal wealth? Could I ever trust my motives for giving to a charity or a street person again?

To quiet my conscience, I used to direct a silent prayer on those rare occasions when I shared my meager wealth with others, asking that any good Karma stemming from the act be cancelled. I know that these prayers took effect because they were asked of the All Highest Father, in the Name of the Christ, and they were closed with three *so be it*'s, one for each aspect of my triune being, instead of with the deadly countermanding "amen". (You, incidentally, can guarantee the efficacy of any unselfish prayer you voice verbally or in thought by following these three vital rules.) But aside from these "cancellation prayers", I assuaged my conscience mostly by not giving anything to anybody.

So from a charity standpoint, things were at an impasse in my life. I suspected I was not properly sharing my wealth because I found my cancellation prayers to be distasteful and hypocritical. But I did not want to give money with the knowledge gnawing at me that I might be giving it for selfish motives — to milk the Universal Larder out of what I knew it would unfailingly give me in return.

So there I stood, and in fact, *there I stand right now, at the present moment, as I write these words.* I am writing this, you see, to exploit another of Creation's most certain Laws. This Law has been working throughout the penning of these little documents. It seems the act of undertaking to explain to others what I have learned on a subject causes any conundrums or quandaries related to the subject, even those which may have hounded me for years, to be resolved!

The quandary we are now addressing is one such quandary, one I long to have solved, and I began this piece solely to get the thing resolved once and for all. When the answer comes forth through these words, you will be seeing it in the exact same context and sequence of thought as I saw it.

And like a novelist who is motivated to finish a novel, even one he may dislike and know to be unsalable, just to see what happens to the characters he has created and set in motion, I am sitting here and writing feverishly to get to the magical spot in this piece where the answer — the Highest Wisdom on the subject — will drop into its proper place and display itself for all of us to see.

And though it is a puzzlement as to why the answer has to be led up to so gradually and obliquely, I think I am just now beginning to see the *drama* of this little tract. It turns out that its primary purpose is to let you, an intimate co-creator of these documents, see firsthand how these things work out. The answering of my question is only the secondary purpose and can therefore wait its time.

But joy of joys! Its turn has finally come! My handwriting is getting large and frantic and scarcely legible, even to me. Chills are actually coursing up and down my spine. I can sense that the Sacred Pool of the Divine Wisdom is about to meet our heartfelt needs once again.

Thank *you*, dear reader. Thank *you*, All That Is, Eternal Fount of the Highest Wisdom. Together, the three of us, who are really *One*, have simply *taken* wealth of Wisdom, even as *one may legitimately take wealth of mammon* by sharing one's present wealth with others! It simply does not matter if one is aware of the Potent Law of Giving, nor if one gives for selfish motives alone.

All we need do is *give*. Even as I started this piece by giving you my store of Wisdom on a subject, a store which of course I was in turn given by others, and in the act of giving out old Wisdom "new" Wisdom was forthcoming to share along with the old, so can we both do the same with mere shekels!

You gain from the act; I gain from the act. It was of no consequence that I began this document solely to exploit a Law which I knew to operate without fail, and to selfishly obtain an answer to a problem that had been haunting me for a long time. The Law still worked!

And so will the Law apply in the giving of money. For it is *one and the same Law*! It is the Law of Giving. It is the Law of Return. It is the One Facet of the Law of Karma, which springs from the Ultimate Law, the Ultimate Principle: *Unity*!

All Ideals, all Laws and Principles, All Truth, All Beauty, and All Wisdom are traceable to this Ultimate of Ultimates, the Highest Truth and the Highest Wisdom: *Unity*!

P.S. This is the first and probably only postscript to any of these tracts, but you will agree that this particular document literally cries out for one.

The logic of the above resolution to my quandary, after I had written it out and had time to think about it, was so clear and natural that I wondered why I could not have reasoned the answer out for myself. After all, when men exploit other Cosmic Laws, physical and otherwise, for their own immediate profit, knowing how the Laws work, does that abrogate the Laws? Could one abrogate the Law of Gravity? The Law of Centrifugal Force? The Laws of the radiation spectrum?

But for some reason I could not see this until just now. Everything I wrote is true, and happened exactly as I said it happened. I assure you of the truth of that statement with the Highest and Most Sacred Oath utterable or writable: In the Name of Unity, our Common Self.

WHAT IS THE COSMIC FORCE?

The Cosmic Force is literally beyond human concept. This is because, among other things, that It *is* the phenomenon which creates human concept, and to understand It from the human point of view would be akin to writing your name to indicate your ownership of a fine gold pen *on* that pen *using* that pen.

And so was born the "mystical" concept. The mystical concept was necessary because otherwise it can be a frustrating undertaking to study and to understand that which underlies such abstract concepts as "studying" and "understanding" as well as concrete objects which might lend themselves to studying and understanding. You can achieve a comprehension of the Cosmic Force only via a mystical viewpoint; i.e., by attempting to align yourself with Its Creator in a mode of Pure Consciousness.

When Jesus of Nazareth gave Voice to the Cosmic Force, he could only say "I am nearer than hands and feet, closer than breathing". When he gave Voice to Its Creator, he could only state: "I and my Father are One". You and I can make the exact same statements with the same degree of truth, because the Cosmic Force, like Its Creator, is One, and no person or no thing can dwell apart from It.

A movement sprang up on Earth in the 1930's which was commonly called the I AM movement. It was a noble attempt by the world teachers to name for human understanding the Cosmic Force. *I AM* is a worthwhile name, for the essence of the Cosmic Force is *identity*. A prominent aspect of the I AM teachings was that human affirmations prefaced by the words *I am* are particularly potent, especially when uttered verbally. This is true, and it is extremely important that we never make casual comments, even in jest, such as "I'm fat", or "I'm really stupid", or "I'm a loser". These statements, if not vigorously countermanded, can have a way of materializing into our reality. The words *I AM* are an excellent synonym for the Cosmic Force, as best depicted when the Israelites were told the name of God: "I AM that I AM".

But in earthly terms, by far the best synonym for the Cosmic Force is *Love*. Not motherly love, or religious adoration, and certainly not the physical lust which promotes such terms as "in love with", but *Love* with the capital letter. Love has been best defined in metaphysical literature as Consciousness seeking to know Itself. And so It is the Source of all identity, the Great I

AM, a *mystical* concept nonpareil.

It is not only your human identity, temporary and fragmentary though that may be, It is also your *Soul* identity. It is also your Soul's Soul identity!

It is likewise the identity of every cell, molecule and atom of your being. Your cells may not be self-conscious — aware of the fact that they are conscious — but they *are* conscious as cells. Similarly, your cat may not be self-conscious, but it *is* aware that it is a cat. This is identity; this is the Cosmic Force. This is I AM, the Creative Consciousness.

We men can lift our species immeasurably by being aware of this Force and Its purpose, and by recognizing It as a Unity — the Force behind all things and all concepts. It is the fount of all Ideas, and I, you, your cat, your car, and its cigarette lighter are naught but Ideas springing from this Source.

To know this Force is of course to love it, using "love" in this sense as affection, respect, adoration. But, and this is a most important point, you can also Love the Cosmic Force in the sense of Creative Love — Consciousness reaching out to know Itself. You can attune your own spark of Divine Consciousness to this Force and, quite surprisingly, actually *augment* It. It is as if you become a stepup transformer of the Force, a relay station for the Divine Energy, when you Love or attune yourself to this Force.

Many people do this subconsciously, or perhaps superconsciously to be more accurate, having learned the technique in prior lives. These are the charismatic people whom you may have met and felt drawn to. These are the people who *radiate*, and who give rise to the terms *radiant health* and *radiant beauty*. Physically, they may be no more healthy or beautiful than you or I, yet in *essence* they are because they have aligned themselves with the Cosmic Force to a greater degree than you or I.

Intellect, physique, or social standing can have no impact on what you may achieve by attuning yourself to the Cosmic Force. What you now read, perhaps with bemusement or skepticism or desultory attentiveness, is the most profound and powerful mystical truth I am capable of sharing with you. To attune yourself with the Divine Love, the Cosmic Force, you need do only two things: (1) convince yourself intellectually of Its omnipresence, of Its nature as the Master Idea from which all phenomena spring, and (2) consciously visualize yourself as a power relay station for Its currents at all times. Step *one* is the easiest step; the rewards begin to flow with step *two*.

You may find yourself becoming a healer, a saint, or a world ruler if you assiduously pursue the exercise of step *two*. But even the most perfunctory invocation of its technique will work minor miracles for you. For one thing, the Cosmic Energy which animates the hierarchy of your being — its organs, cells, molecules, atoms, and sub-atomic light particles — will be enhanced to the point where you literally can clear any obstruction of any duration, no matter what its cumulative damage to your physical system may be.

Laughter and good humor, as Norman Cousins discovered, can be a powerful tool for aligning yourself with the Cosmic Force. But a deep, abiding joy in the fact that the Force *is*, that It is a unifying Force that embraces All That Is including your human consciousness, and that Its infinite power is free for the asking, is capable of working more miraculous cures than Mr. Cousins ever dreamed possible.

This Force can not only transform you and your reality, It can transform the World Reality if as few as two or three of us unite in directing It. And there you have the explanation to yet another mystical statement: "Where two or more are gathered in my name, there I Am".

RADIATING THE COSMIC FORCE

The conscious wielding — the voluntary radiation of the Cosmic Force by us — is a most potent and extremely effective exercise. It exploits the Law of Giving in that it guarantees us a greater flow of this Force through our beings, just as the Law of Giving when applied to wealth of money or wealth of Wisdom guarantees more money and greater Wisdom.

It is curious how we men can observe this Law of Giving at work when it comes to physical energy, but cannot extrapolate the Law to Its workings in other areas within the Universal cornucopia. We know that the more sedentary and inactive we are, the more listless and unenergetic we feel. And we find that when we *use* physical energy by way of an exercise program or simply by getting up and doing something, there seems to be a great deal more energy available to us. Yet common though this knowledge be, no one seems to question the inner workings of this phenomenon.

When you channel the Force from the core of your being, from your heart of hearts, through your body in a radiating pattern and out into the Cosmos through every pore in your skin, through every cell, *through every atom*, you are giving back to the Cosmos your private allotment of Light. It does not matter to whom nor to what part of the Cosmos you pour out your Light, you are giving back the Light to the Cosmos. And inevitably, the Law of Giving guarantees that you will be given enough Light to replace that which you have given, plus a great deal more.

If you can radiate forth your Light at least once daily, but preferably three times per day for a brief while, you will feel yourself growing progressively lighter in weight. It is tempting to conjecture if it was not indeed by Divine plan that the English word *light* means freedom from gravity as well as absence of darkness. For most assuredly, the more enlightened a human being, the freer he is from the hold of the grave — the grave of the living dead — the grave of we who call ourselves the "living".

As you feel lighter in weight, your body will also develop an ehtereal feeling about it — a vaguely "unreal" feeling — frothy and flighty. This will be a sign you are awakening your ethereal body and are constructing a physical body using matter of the ethereal plane. And as this body is built and you are primed to awaken in it, you will come to realize most vividly that The Divine One is...Consciousness!

Consciousness is the Only Thing That Is. It is that which unites us all because It *is* us all. These are most vital facts that you will gradually come to see quite clearly, and you will see other facts in a way that you cannot imagine intellectually. You will know these facts within every atom of your being because every atom of your being is a hologram of Infinite Creation — the Cosmos literally being contained within any one given atom of Creation. On any plane of being, the atom has the seeds of a universe as complex as, and in fact identical to, the Universe which houses you and me and that atom — and that galaxy cluster 300 billion light-years away.

When you have directed the Divine Fire from within the Permanent Atom of your being out to and into each and every atom of your body, then to each and every atom of the Unvierse, you have showered Light upon trillions of mini-cosmoses. The Light will be reflected back unto you, entering into your heart of hearts through the same route it exited — the atoms of your physical body. Only now It has been enhanced, for It has been propelled back to you with the Force of a trillion trillion recipients, each pregnant with your potential for the projection of the Holy Fire.

And then will true grace befall you. This Force can work miracles even in small quantities — even in soft-focus — so it tittilates the imagination to ponder what It can be capable of in such mass quantities. You can literally be transformed, elevated to the consciousness of your Immortal Self. And it all will be due to Consciousness — the Holy One — which can so easily manifest as atoms or men or grasshoppers and see Itself through their eyes.

HOW TO BE A HEALER

Anyone can be a healer simply by willing it through the act of visualization. To will it through visualization, you simply see in your mind's eye a warm, healing fire arising from deep within your breast, then flowing out through every pore of your skin so that you *radiate*. This is what is usually meant when people are said to be in *radiant* good health, or when *radiant beauty* is the term used to describe a very rare and exalted beauty. People who are blessed with radiant good health or radiant beauty are people who consciously or subconsciously channel this sacred fire through and out their physical bodies. This fire is a functioning of the Divine Force, a portion that manifests on the physical plane of existence. This awesome Force, freely available for our manipulation, should only be used for good — in the service of the Divine Will. If used for evil, it will destroy the individual who thus channels it.

When we awaken this Sacred Force within us, we first heal ourselves. Then we can focus It to heal others, concentrating and directing it outward through the palms of the hands and the tips of the fingers and thumbs.

This has been practiced for so long and by so many humans, that it seems fatuous to have to document the truth of this healing Force and of humans' ability to exploit it. All of the "magic' which stems from the laying-on-of-hands and the massage and accupressure schools of healing is due mostly to this force and the belief of the practitioner that he or she can wield it. The country doctors whose mere touch makes us feel better are humble channels of this Force.

Again, anyone — *anyone* — whose intentions are honorable, and who wants to alleviate human suffering to any extent whereby it does not interfere with the Divine Will, can serve as a channel for this Force and become a healer. When you do so, do not just pour healing rays upon and into the afflicted. This will provide immediate relief and cure for a current ailment, but it will not help the inevitable future ailments. Teach your beneficiaries to do what you do — to channel the sacred fire in a positive, loving manner, showering it out upon all Creation. If you can convince them of the ease of doing this, you will have healed them for life and will have created a new healer to help you help the world.

If afflicted, we are the source of our afflictions. They may be due to thoughts and actions of bygone ages, but they are still our personal liability — no external force visits them upon us. Divine Grace may send to us a human who has learned to heal, but if we do not change our thoughts and thus our actions, we will only be subject to re-affliction. And oddly enough, the act of channeling the Love Force through and out our bodies serves to protect our thoughts from negative influences, and therefore helps purify our thoughts. And it also casts a physical glow about our bodies that strengthens and protects every cell, every molecule, every atom of our beings.

You can heal anyone you come in contact with, whether stranger or intimate loved one. Merely channel the Force into them. Then teach them to do as you do. Then channel your Forces in tandem in a general healing of Earth and all of her creatures and creations — from mountains to aardvarks to orchids. Feel yourselves lifting Earth up with the Divine Fire as rocket fuel. Feel yourselves spinning a web of protection around her using the silk of the Divine Fire.

The color which should be envisioned during healing efforts is *violet*.

WHAT ROLE DID JESUS REALLY PLAY FOR MAN?

Jesus of Nazareth dedicated his life to fulfill the necessary drama of the highly mystical Passion Play, an allegory of the necessary steps a man must follow on the road to salvation — "salvation" being nothing but a re-awakening to his true estate and a spiritual, mental, and physical identification with Unity. Not only was and is Jesus the Life Projector and Reality Monitor of his own allegorical life, but he was also the earthly vehicle for Earth's direct contact with a Being of a high, high order, a Being whom we call the Christ.

Temporarily, this Being is the highest Creative Father of whom most men are capable of conceiving. He unites us all in Unity, and to be aware of your oneness with Him is commonly called "Christ Consciousness" by esoterically-minded Christians, and "cosmic consciousness" by esoterically-minded non-Christians. Achieving this state of consciousness, which has been done by many men, is said to be a more joyous event than one can imagine. Even when it comes "accidentally" — by Grace, actually — and fleetingly to a man, darting away after a moment's illumination, the adorned creature is changed forever and for the better. The briefest glimpse of this consciousness has caused men to lose all fear of death, to see that death is an illusion that Man created for his own purposes and that he in no way need enslave himself to that illusion. The slightest whiff of the cosmic consciousness aroma will infuse those whom it graces with a deep, abiding joy. This joy is spawned by a brief awareness of the Unity of All Things, and an indelible memory of how Real and True that brief awareness was.

But those whom it briefly and unpredictably graces are not always aware of the fact that they can attain that consciousness *permanently*. It need not be a fleeting thing, a blissful vista never to be seen again. It can and should be and *will* be Man's true estate. Not his highest estate possible, for there are intensities of spirits even greater than the Christ Spirit — even those which embrace the Christ Spirit and perhaps other Spirits like It — for the Omniverse is a pyramidal gestalt, to use Seth's term. Man's highest possible estate will come in the day that he stands aware of the All Highest Father, the Center of His Being, the Infinite One.

So Jesus of Nazareth's most vital service to Man was

rendered when he put his small self aside and gave voice to our unifying Spirit, the Christ Consciousness. Other men have done this, but apparently the effects from Jesus' self-sacrifice were so much more pronounced and had such a lasting impact because the event was part and parcel of the mystical allegory portrayed by Jesus' life.

The Voice which spoke to us via Jesus' mortal lips showed us a Spirit of infinite compassion, infinite love, and infinite Wisdom. Much of what It spoke has of course been lost to us in historical terms, and yet because the drama is an ongoing one and will not conclude until the Second Coming, we cannot really use the term "lost" in any context with this powerful Mystery. But what did survive to the best of our knowledge reveals an Ideal for all men to aspire to: an Ideal known best as Man's True Self, or Christ Self.

This Ideal bespeaks Nobility. It is nobility of Spirit, nobility of Consciousness, and nobility of behavior. It is Eternal Truth made manifest: the sacrifice of the false self to Unity, the return of the Prodigal Son to his ancient home.

And you may well ask: what purpose does it serve to know this, assuming it be true, aside from satisfaction of idle curiosity? The answer of course is that it serves no purpose to those without a need. But to those who feel a need to be free of the grave, to those who yearn to get off of the carousel, to those who are weary of death and decay and impermanence, the service rendered by the Passion Play and by the utterances of the Most High and Sacred Voice will provide the threefold answer: who they are, where they are going, and how to get there.

JUMP ON THE SILVER EXPRESS

A vital and productive technique for those of you who can accept and believe beyond doubt that the Highest Truth is Unity, is a technique that leads to what can best be termed as "A Ride on the Silver Express".

This technique requires only a mental effort on your part, although a little emotional energy will not hurt and in fact will act as a booster for whatever mental energy is put forth. This technique requires that you mentally visualize that the vast store of Cosmic Energy given you for your personal use in the fashioning of the Universe, this awesome depository of energy deep within you, is being summoned up by you. You are calling it forth from within the inner core of your being, and you are focusing it on the Divine Stream of Energy which works for the All Highest Good. By so focusing, your personal energy allotment is blended with the Pure Stream, the Will of the All Highest Father.

This Pure Stream of Cosmic Love and Energy, with which you should blend your personal love and energy, is called the Silver Express. When you are in sync with It, It produces a natural high which you will not be likely to ever forget. It can produce flashes and waves of cosmic consciousness, using the term in the sense that Bucke used it. It can even lead to self-awakening.

But no matter how startling its immediate effects may be, its long-term effects are even more unbelievable. Riding the Silver Express, even occasionally, will eventually bring an order and sense of direction to your life and to the events which mould it. Literally, you will quit marking time and will get on with the business that you were sent here to attend to. You might not necessarily know consciously what steps to take in your life, but you will be guided adeptly by circumstance. Or perhaps you *will* know consciously what to do at all times because you may be placed in touch with the Inner Voice. You will hear Its whispers of Wisdom and good judgment, and you will obey It. But usually, you will just be led automatically into doing whatever it is you are supposed to do in keeping with the All Highest Good. It may mean suffering or ignominy, but you will accept what comes your way peacefully and with courage because you know somehow that you are now in tune with the Cosmic Will, the Will of God. Such is the potency of this technique, this "riding the Silver express", that it brings peace and serenity to doorsteps where no man would believe peace and serenity could ever approach.

While mentally focusing your energy along the path of God's Will, an already powerful and intense Pure Stream, you will oddly enough *enhance* that Stream and intensify It even further. Your efforts can be accompanied by words if you wish. The spoken vow or prayer can be most efficacious with this technique. The Lord's Prayer, specifically the verse "Thy Kingdom come, Thy Will be done, in Earth as it is in Heaven", is a worthwhile phrase to repeat during this exercise

And as things happen to you after you have practiced this technique for awhile, whether good things or "bad" things, you will say to your Inner Self: "In all things give thanks...". And you will automatically remember the Silver Express, and how it is whisking you along with It as It travels into a monk's life, or into a blade of grass, or out from the center of the Great Central Sun, and out from the core of your being, forming Ideas and Thoughts and Reality. And knowing that this One Pure Stream is the Only Thing That Is, the I Am That I Am, the Alpha and the Omega, the Living Christ, the Ultimate Deity, you will joyously go along with It.

And eventually, you will be transformed.

HOW TO CONQUER ANXIETY

Unlike fear, anxiety has a nameless and usually non-existent object. Anxiety is otherwise the same as fear.

Fear occurs when confronting a mugger, or attacking with the infantry, or facing surgery. There is a concrete threat: nameable and definitely existent.

Anxiety is the same emotion, usually not as intense, but instead directed at an imaginary host of events with no substance at all to them except for what anxiety's sufferer cares to give them. If you know the whys and wherefores of anxiety, you can conquer it.

Anxiety stems from an awareness of mortality. That is why it afflicts older people more than younger people, and grows more intense with advancing age. The older we become, the more real an imagined "end" called death becomes to us. And as this awareness hits us, we realize that something — some disease, some accident, some cataclysmic event — is going to be our downfall. And so every disease or accident or cataclysmic event we read about becomes a candidate for our "angel of death". For some people the favorite becomes nuclear war; for others it may be cancer or heart disease or Alzheimer's disease. For others it may not center on any one catastrophe but instead may just be a fear of a possible accident, a fear which in its greatest intensity produces agorophobia. But we "know" that we are mortal and we therefore "know" that something has to "end" our lives.

Even little children can be stricken with anxiety when they first become aware of mortality. Fortunately, they are so caught up with life and living that they soon forget their awareness of their own mortality, and thus their fear of that host of events which are capable of ending their lives.

Unless a young person of 35 years or less has been subjected to one or more deaths of those close to him, he is unlikely to be aware of his mortality and thus is unlikely to suffer from anxiety. Otherwise, the awareness of one's own mortality almost always occurs somewhere between 35 and 45 years of age. The people who do not succumb to the anxiety which stems from this trauma of realization, or who may succumb temporarily but quickly overcome it, are those who have followed one of several courses. At least one of these techniques for the defeat of anxiety will work for you should you care to try them.

The easiest course is to realize that *you are not alone* in your current mental state. Some people are capable of enormous courage when they face a danger in common with others — this is especially true of the warrior caste, those natural-born soldiers. If you are of this persuasion, you can conquer fear of death when you realize that everyone around you — fathers and mothers, brothers and sisters, sons and daughters — are up against the same enemy. The enemy may be a myth, true, but all of you collectively believe in him, and so he becomes real. And he will conquer you *only if you so will it*! But whether you believe that statement or not, you still may be able to eliminate your fear of death through the realization that you indeed have ample company.

Another course you can follow in conquering anxiety is to revert to your childhood technique for anxiety banishment — live life to the fullest, live life vibrantly, and love life to the extinction of death. Many people have used this technique in their later age, and we owe the spirit of volunteerism to those who practice this method of anxiety elimination. When you work energetically on behalf of others, you tend to forget your personal self and thus your own mortality, for it is only your false personal self, or small self, who is mortal. Your True Self, the Divine Force Behind All, is of course immortal. And your *true personal self*, your soul, is of course immortal. So whether a person becomes aware of these higher selves or not is immaterial: he or she can conquer anxiety simply by living vibrantly for others and forgetting his or her small personal self.

Another good method, widely used to great success, is to focus attention on your true personal self, the soul, which being immortal renders you impervious to anxiety. All of the routine Western religions can help you in the pursuit of this path. In fact, this path probably would not exist were it not for our earthly religions. They are indeed the noble servants of Man, even if they are nothing but the inventions of Man. They are gifts of the gods because *men are gods*! They are to be respected at all times. If your goal is to conquer anxiety and if no other method works for you, this one most certainly will.

The last method for conquering anxiety is the best method, for when it works it is always a *permanent* victory. The other courses, usually temporary in that they work with this particular mortal manifestation of yourself, your "current" life, can nevertheless on occasion become permanent. A saintly presence who lifts others by her exalted service to Man — someone such as

Mother Teresa — can literally transcend the trap of mortality through her impact on her fellow humans, and the end of her current mortal round can see a graduation to her True Estate, the Heavenly Kingdom spoken of in the New Testament. Other saints can transcend themselves in their love for their religious idol; they actually *expand* their selves through the pouring out of the Universal Love which boils and bubbles within the hearts of each one of us. This same technique can just as easily render permanent conquering of death by being directed at Ideals other than religious ideals. Great love for the Universal Love Force or for any of its Eternal Concepts is an almost surefire way to permanently conquer that false concept called "death". Love of Wisdom, love of Creativity, love of Humanity — that highest and most masterful expression of the Human Spirit — all such love of Ideals, when showered forth in great streams from deep within your being, will lift you up permanently out of mortality. Most specifically, love of the One True Being Himself will be the most efficacious Ideal for you to radiate your love toward. This love of Unity, of All That Is, is also a love of yourself, you being a most noble manifestation of All That Is — the Heavenly Father — the Divine One. Such love is a love of everything and everyone as a manifestation of the One. It is a love for the Ideal of all Ideals, the Idea behind all Ideas, the All Highest Father.

So even though the other methods for conquering anxiety and the fear of death may yield permanent results when practiced to near-perfection, those of us who are incapable of perfection should take the best course, the course which *always* yields a permanent conquering of anxiety. It does so because the method is, quite simply, the *conquering of death*.

When you conquer death, you never face anxiety again throughout the eternity of your existence. When you conquer death, you return to your True Estate. All of the examples of the permanent conquering of anxiety mentioned above derived their permanence from this one phenomenon: the conquering of death.

Throughout history, men have utilized this method for the defeat of anxiety. The mystery schools put men on an initiatory path whereby their higher selves were refined and awakened through techniques handed down and refined over countless eons — there truly being nothing new under the Sun. The mystery school technique for death conquering has never been a heavily used path for men because it usually requires many lives to be ready for the schools, and then several more lives under their tutelage before one can complete all of the initiations. There have been exceptions, of course, but this has been the norm.

A more commonly attempted method for the conquering of death, albeit not nearly as commonly successful, is world withdrawal — monkhood or hermitage. This technique works only when it leads to a total awareness of The One. The reason the ascetic, hermited, unworldly path so seldom can lead to an awareness of The One is that the act of withdrawing from this world is a form of withdrawal from The One — the world being naught but a colossally complex and beautiful manifestation of The One! The hermit or monk is thus confronted with the necessity of travelling west to arrive at a nearby destination to the east. It can be done, but it can also be a most difficult trek.

Other people have conquered death through Divine Grace; through a belief in It and a great love for It. It is of course real. It has saved many people from mortality. It is among the highest manifestations — perhaps even the *highest* manifestation — of the Holy Mother, the Celestial Virgin. Divine Grace is the act of enfolding oneself into The One: one's consciousness, one's feelings, and one's body. The body is literally *lifted* to its permanent estate by this enfoldment into The One. Divine Grace is most easily obtained by a great love for the Divine Mother — the feminine polarity of Creation, the first and foremost offspring of the Divine Father. The product of Their consort is the Son — Creation as we know It — Spirit going into Form to make Itself known to Itself — the Living Christ, the Loving Christ — blazing glory upon glory in realms we cannot yet even dream of but which we will surely come to know.

If you appeal for Divine Grace to the Holy Mother, in whatever form you can best conceive of Her, your appeal shall be heard and answered. Therefore this can be a ridiculously easy method for the conquering of death and the permanent erasement of anxiety.

Another method for conquering death presents itself only on rare occasions, and you might therefore classify it itself as a *form* of Divine Grace. It occurs once every 25,000 years or so when Earth undergoes a polar shift. It is a predictable event throughout the Cosmos and therefore attracts volunteers to our planet who come in a loving journey of assistance which they usually term "the harvest". They know that a major portion of our planet's inhabitants are about to be lost to physical existence and that indeed if it were not for their help *all* of our planet's inhabitants would be thus lost. And so they congregate in the vicinity of Earth, arriving from various planes and planets throughout the local universe, awaiting and preparing for the harvest. When you read of the harvest in the New Testament, this is the harvest being referred to. When you read of the resurrection of the dead, this is what is being referred to since in New Testatment terminology "the dead" are we who call ourselves "the living". Our mortal state is *death* compared to our normal state. The term is exactly appropriate and is in no wise meant to confuse.

Because these volunteers who serve Man are of the highest moral development and are true devotees of Unity — the All Highest Father — they manifest a Christlike appearance to mortals in their demeanor, speech, and philosophy. They therefore are often referred to as Christ Spirits, or Servants of Christ, or the Christ Force. They come here to serve on all occasions of crisis, not just when polar shifts impend, but they come in greatest numbers and from the highest levels when a cataclysm on the order of the polar shift is imminent, as it now is.

They can be your salvation, as salvation is spoken of in the New Testament. They can literally "take you up to heaven", and they will indeed do this for "the chosen". If you are a worthy candidate for salvation, they will of necessity save you. Some of you already know of our visitors and their mission by having read of them elsewhere. Others of you know by intuition, a subconscious knowledge planted in you before birth. Because of the ease with which we can enlist the services of our helpers, we are forced to regard them as manifestations of the Divine Grace.

It was Grace which placed you here in life on Earth at this particular time, and it is Grace which has led you to the words you now read. All you need do now is replace fear with Love, and replace hate with Trust. You need only resolve not to be frightened by, nor show animosity toward, any being — earthly or nonearthly. This means literally that you must beat your sword into a plowshare, that you cease to contend with your fellow man over any matter, and most especially over mammon. It means that you adopt the spirit of loving service shown by our visitors, the members of the Christ Force. To travel in the company of a group means that you must adopt the culture and manners of that group! They literally cannot take with them any individual who is still caught in the throes of earthman barbarity, for were they to approach such a one he or she would flee in terror!

As it stands, most of those who flee will perforce flee to their immediate physical doom. Some of Earth's citizens will be physically saved to propagate the race, but they will survive only to taste of death 30 or 40 or 50 years later. The permanent salvation spoken of in the bible means that the saved will have to be one with the Christ Force, and to step willingly, fearlessly, and lovingly into the craft of the Christ Force when so invited. You can easily do this if you start right now learning to love all things on all planes of existence. Try to understand what Unity is — how vast and noble and beautiful It is — and how much of It is unknown to you. Trust in the tender benevolence of Unity and It will shower Its benevolences on you.

Be contrite and humble in your ignorance. Bear no ill will; bear only good will towards all men and nations and races. See yourself in others, for verily there you most certainly are! See others in yourself; see God in yourself; Love yourself.

Become a citizen of the Cosmos, ready to be of service to the All Highest Good. Dedicate your personal will to the Divine Will. Worship the highest spirit in Man, and give thanks to the Universal Love Force for all things.

Love Wisdom, which is nothing but the spiritual truth of All Things. Love Creation! You need not become a saint, but you *must* show yourself worthy of being harvested when the Christ Force approaches Earth! This is why you are here. This is the time of the great testing.

The chosen shall be chosen by — of all people — *themselves*!

YOU FIND WHAT YOU WORSHIP

If you worship Beauty, Beauty will present Herself to you wherever you turn. You will be constantly led to or exposed to awesome sights of Beauty.

If you worship Wisdom, you will be led to the heart of every matter — the Highest Wisdom of the matter — and It too will present Itself to you wherever you may turn your attention.

And if you worship the One, the Father of Hosts, the Infinite Creator, then too shall Unity present Itself to you at every opportunity. You will be constantly reminded with each thought that that thought is a part of the Whole, created with the Precious Stuff of Consciousness, and that it therefore affects the Whole, either lifting it up with a positive orientation or holding it back with a negative orientation.

Your responsibility for your thoughts will be constantly borne home to you. You will come to be intolerant of idle, wandering, aimless thoughts and you will constantly come to feel a need to think something positive and worthwhile, to help advance the upward evolution of All That Is. The best thought you can hold if none others present themselves is this one: "In all things give thanks". This thought will remind you that the Will of the All Highest Father is constantly being done through you.

As a man thinks, so does he act. If you think of the Father's Will at all times, silently praying "Thy will by done" whenever faced with decisions, even those of mundane proportions, then eventually you will become an active agent of the Father's Will, and soon your own personal will shall subordinate itself to the Will for the All Highest Good. This prayer — "Thy will be done" — and this thought — "In all things give thanks" — will lead you towards a merging of your will with the Divine Will. It is inevitable that you will have to achieve this merger some day, so you might as well make things easier for yourself and achieve the merger as soon as possible.

A critical juncture in Earth's history is about to appear in time, and it is of importance for all of you who read these words to pause and give thought to whether you will be judged among the quick or the dead, for the day of judgment of the living dead is about to dawn. Those who will have no more of death and decay will have an opportunity to help lift Earth into a higher realm where these phenomena do not exist. Others will have the opportunity to escape mortality itself permanently, on all planes of being, and to return to their heavenly estates in the Kingdom of the Father. Their mansions await them; they awaken on a golden summer's dawn with exquisite scents of dew and blossoms, serenaded by music designed to transport the living soul to ecstasy. And lo! on awakening they find that they were home all the while! It was only a bad dream, a subtle trap that was laid by past actions, a trap within which each returnee ensnared himself.

For Man, as offspring of Gods, is himself a God. A sleeping God, a God totally unaware, yet nonetheless a God. And so it is painful in the extreme to see men afraid to be themselves, slavishly miming the actions and speech and beliefs of whomever they deem their "leaders". It is painful also to see men whiling away their lives in trivial entertainments, trying to forget that they are "going to die". If they believe it, it is true. As Gods, they can and do constantly create their own realities, and whatever they believe to be true has a pernicious way of becoming true, if only to them.

So if men believe their consciousness is trapped in their flesh and cannot sojourn away from it, then it is true. And worse, if they believe that their consciousness *is* their fleshly body or vice versa, then to them it is true! Whatsoever men choose to perceive *is*, and whatever *is* is real and eternally valid, for nothing exists but Consciousness playing upon Form, the Ether, and creating events and situations and characters and plots and dialogs.

It is all a Game, a bright and loving and somewhat mischievous Game. It is a brilliant, blazing Diamond of an infinite number of glittering facets, each facet containing a Rainbow of Creation within a Rainbow within a Rainbow. It is Creation Itself. It is All That Is. It is *That I Am*. And when higher beings spoke to the Hebrews in the guise of God to tell them the Name of God, they said correctly — as God would say were He to speak on the subject — I Am That I Am.

God is That I Am — Creation — Self-consciousness and Cosmic Consciousness — Matter and Spirit — a Trinity of manifestation on seven levels of being — Unity! Acknowledge, then worship, your place in this boundless flow of Energy. Align yourself with It in Its natural direction. Pray constantly "Thy will be done" and think constantly "In all things give thanks". And soon your will and the Will of the All Highest Father will be One.

You find what you worship.

PRISONERS OF INTELLECT

It has occurred to me that someone might take issue with the definition of Wisdom as given herein on several occasions. (For those who may have forgot, Wisdom is Intelligence — Consciousness — applied to spiritual matters. Wisdom is also the spiritual Truth of any matter. In other words, Wisdom is always the product, the sum, and the dividend of the combined actions of Intellect and Spirit, no matter in what juxtaposition.) Those who take issue might be great intellects who consider themselves to be also wise, but who nevertheless hold no truck with Spirit. They would therefore consider themselves living testimony to the falsity of the Higher Wisdom's definition of Wisdom, as recapitulated above.

But if there are such creatures in our audience — and I admit that it would be highly unlikely if there *were* — and if they do *truly* not believe in Spirit, I would say to them that it is impossible for them to be wise. There has never been a man of Wisdom, and there never *will* be a man of Wisdom, who does not accredit Spirit. When evaluating the truth of that statement, be sure to remember that some men claim to be atheists who are merely agnostics or pantheists or whatever, and so they indeed are believers in Spirit, even if only in the Spirit of Man.

There are even men who believe in the Spirit of Man but who probably do not know it. Those who may be drawn to a sympathy with Jung's "collective unconscious" and "universal archtypes" are believers in the Spirit of Man, for those phenomena are part and parcel with Spirit. In fact, *they are Spirit!*

For what else do you think Spirit is? It is Consciousness in Action. It is also known as Love, with the capital "L". It is First Cause. And It is the effect of that Cause — *you*! You and all other Creatures of First Cause, from the Atom "up", are possessed of Spirit because you were created by Spirit. You have consciousness because you were created by Consciousness.

You are God because you were created by God! And after creating you, His first offspring, He found that He could not create anything whatsoever that was outside of Him, nor anything whatsoever that did not contain Him!

Now since we have started referring to Spirit as *God*, perhaps we can understand who God really is, and why some people say "God is Love" and others say "God is Consciousness". There are even a few who will say "God is Spirit". He is all of these and He is also you and every other projection of Consciousness, for He is quite simply All That Is.

Do you now see why it is said that "no man can see God and live"? Such a man would be God, not man, if he could see Himself in His totality. For God, the Ancient of Days, is the Supreme Intelligence, the Greatest Knower and Experiencer of Creation known to us. And yet it is suspected by some very High Intelligences that even *He* is transcended by Those more ancient!

The Universal Larder of Wisdom, that most Holy Fount, cannot be approached nor supped from by those who do not believe in Spirit because *It is Spirit*! The non-believers, the dialectical materialists, do not comprehend the fortress they have built around themselves, for they — not Spirit — have erected the barricades keeping them from the Sacred Fount. Do they have even an inkling of an idea of what knowledge, what creative insights, they are denying themselves? The psychic pain which prisoners of intellect must endure is beyond the comprehension of us more normal people. Can you imagine the degree of anxiety that *they* must be afflicted with? But even aside from psychic pain, can you imagine the darkness of the world in which they dwell? It cannot be penetrated by Light, for *Light is also synonymous with Spirit*! What agony it must be for them to know the facts of everything and the Truth of nothing.

Pray for these unfortunate ones, for there are many among them who can be moved by Divine Grace if there be someone somewhere to invoke Her for them. Those prisoners of intellect who in the past have been saved were saved by the Most Holy Grace, and it was either due to their good Karma or to the prayers of someone who cared about them. Pray for them no matter how they may abuse or mock you for your Spiritual orientation. Indeed, if they are supercilious toward, or show contempt for your belief in Spirit in any manner, they are then most worthy of your prayers for two reasons: (1) they are the ones who are most capable of being freed from their prisons by Divine Grace, and (2) the greatest and sweetest revenge you can get should you be offended by their mockery is their conversion, for it is after conversion that they will feel the most agonizing shame for their past attitudes and intellectual pride.

A classic example of a person whom we all know who might fit this category of "intellectual prisoners begging for rescue" would be the comedian and cinema *auteur*, Woody Allen. Now I personally suspect that Woody, deep down inside, is a great believer in Spirit, albeit a Spirit he may be unable to define. But on the surface, at least, he intimates he is *not* and he has occasionally fashioned jokes at the expense of sincere and humble believers in Spirit. He may be like the "lady who doth protest too much" — in reality a seeker of God who delays finding Him for as long as possible to render the conversion all the more sweet. For it is a verity that the longer one endures pain, the greater the bliss when the pain is brought to its end. This is a common masochistic trait, and by way of some of his movie scripts Woody has indicated masochistic tendencies on his part.

But Woody Allen, if he has not already indeed been saved — as I suspect he has — will eventually be rescued from his prison even if no one bothers to pray for him. For it is a basic right and privilege of the Artists among us that they who fall prisoner to their intellects and are thus robbed of Spirit shall be saved by an act of Holy Grace. It is their reward for suffering the bonds of flesh on our behalf. For Artists are lovers — even atheistic Artists — else they could not create, and thus would they not be Artists.

So study carefully the manifestations of a man's true beliefs — his words and his acts — before you proclaim him a man of Wisdom. If they are not resonant with Spirit or with Love or with Consciousness or with God, they are not and they cannot be words or acts of Wisdom. But absence of Wisdom in any creature does not imply an absence of Spirit or spiritual belief. The Angels are among the most spiritual of all Evolutionary Orders, and their basic function is as messengers, but how often are they bearers of Wisdom? It does happen; in fact, for all I know it could be an Angel or Angels who are bringing the Wisdom that you now read. I only know that the Wisdom gets to me somehow, thence to you, and it could be that I am but the penultimate link in a long line of messengers, you of course being the last link.

So just as the absence of intellect cannot forestall Wisdom — there having been many wise fools among us — neither can absence of Wisdom forestall Greatness of Spirit or Greatness in Love or Greatness in Consciousness or Greatness in God-worship. Some of the saints and martyrs have far exceeded the spirituality of the most notable sages. Who would dare compare Mother Teresa or the Apostles Peter or John to the sages Socrates or Plato or Shakespeare for Greatness in Spirit?

Wisdom is not All That Is; there are many equally important and even more important things. But love of Wisdom can be most beneficial to those who choose not to take the sainthood path to God. Wisdom can show you the other paths, and even give instructions on how to tread them. It can lead you intelligently to Spirit, for it *is* the combined action of Spirit and Intelligence. And most important, it can set you free should you be one of the prisoners of intellect.

If you love Wisdom, you are automatically marked as a lover of Spirit, of Love, of Consciousness, and of God.

THE TRUTH ABOUT UFO'S

And now we come to a point where we pick up a Truth that no one person on Earth knows in its entirety: the "bottom line" on the UFO story. As always, I myself do not know the final Truth of this issue, but I do know that the Truth has not been found and coherently published as such by any one person or group. The various people and groups with UFO interests have given truthful explanations and opinions, but they also have given conflicting ones. And often their data is incomplete; they freely admit that they do not know the UFO's purpose, or whether or not they are "multi-dimensional" in our terms, travelling through hyperspace for vast distances to get here, or travelling *in* hyperspace to reach us from higher planes of being, planes that we would commonly refer to as "spiritual".

No one seems to have the definitive answers to these two key questions about UFO's, so it is hoped that we achieve these answers sometime within this document, clearly and with loving compassion for our earthling curiosity. For you see, we have a right to know this data in as unambiguous terms as possible. Curiosity alone is highly pardonable in any creature, it being the very essence of the manifest universe — indeed, the *very reason the manifest universe came into being!* The curiosity of Holy Spirit to be aware of and to understand what It is capable of led to our very existence and to our Reality, however we may perceive it. It led, quite simply, to Creation. This thing called curiosity is indeed the impetus for Love — the Living Christ — which unites you as both creator and observer of Reality, so that you can see Reality as it was meant to be. The True Reality is meant to be, and is, the Will for the All Highest Good. The divinely-willed Reality of the All Highest Father is the Reality we want to perceive.

So we know our curiosity is forgiven us, it being the most basic aspect of Holy Spirit. Thus, questions born of curiosity are by Divine Fiat to be answered. This is a Law and a Principle Concept of Creation. But even aside from curiosity, we have yet another highly valid reason to know the bottom line of the UFO story. It is, after all, our home — Earth — which is being visited, and every host has the right to know his guest's purpose for an uninvited visit. If the reason is "we were just in the neighborhood and thought we'd drop by", then assumedly we will have to accept that answer since we firmly believe that the answer will be a truthful one. But it is a rude guest who does not proffer the explanation for his surprise visit immediately upon arrival, and who forces the host to solicit the reason directly.

So there we have two powerful and undeniable reasons why we are OWED the truth of the UFO matter. Quite simply, the data cannot be denied us. All we need do is take it. So if you will do the reading at the Fount of Wisdom, I will once again enscribe what you read. You can begin now.

No matter where Wisdom or Knowledge or Truth come from, or what route they take to get to you, they come from the Eternal Father. No matter where or from whom you receive a helping hand, it is the Unity of Creation which sends you the help. In all respects your life is ruled by God, for He inspires the bearers of good tidings and the Good Samaritans and the annointed teachers. All good comes from God. The words *God* and *good* are synonymous; it is no accident that they are separated in our language of record by but one letter.

So regardless of a UFO's origins, be it a material world in the material plane that earthmen inhabit, or a higher, more spiritual plane, it comes to you from God, and it comes to you as a great act of *compassion* — compassion of the highest order.

The UFO occupants come from many planes of being, including the three-dimensional plane of Earth, and they are all here to help earthmen through the highly predictable polar shift. It is a major event in the Cosmos when any planet undergoes such a physical cataclysm, but on most planets the residents are quite capable of helping themselves through the ordeal. Earth makes an important event even more important due to her quarantined state, brought about by the barbarity of her inhabitants. Thus a great deal of help from the Cosmic Citizenry — on *all* planes of being — is necessitated. Spiritual assistance is needed; material assistance is required. And due to the high moral character of the vast majority of earthman's Cosmic brothers, they are most eager and deeply honored to participate in any effort which will dramatically lift men up, both spirtually and physically.

And there you have the reason for your garbled prophecies regarding Armageddon, such as the destruction of Earth's "wicked". It is true: the "wicked" will perish in the cataclysm, for they will not be saved by virtue of their own attitudes and volition. And consider the "saved" ones, who are to be "taken up into the heavens". These are the stock for the new, purified, civilization of Earth. Only the pure in heart, the lovers and respectors of Unity, need apply.

Also ponder the "harvest" of souls, those who will be "taken up into *Heaven*". These too are the believers in, and lovers of, Unity. But these are also the awakened ones, the practitioners of Unity, ready to be transported to their True Estate, bypassing the death experience via the Rainbow Bridge of the UFO fleet.

UFO's have helped earthmen in the past; the evidence of their help as outlined in the Holy Bible and in far more ancient religious texts is irrefutable. They are and have been earthman's helpers, his guides, his shepherds for countless centuries. They intervene in Earth's affairs only in accordance with the Will for the All Highest Good. Like earthmen, they are not all of them perfect; they can and do commit blunders on occasion. But *never* have they made mistakes of temperament! Never have they harmed a human being! Whenever ancient texts indicate that a UFO or its powers were used for slaying humans or for wantonly destroying their property, it has been due to *human command of the ships!* Thus it has been ages since the mistake of letting Man have access to a ship or its powerplant has been made, and that mistake will never be made again with this current civilization. Man is so depraved that he will inevitably and immediately turn the most powerful knowledge and the most inspired tools into weapons for the destruction and conquest of his fellow man. The early UFO servants, quite simply, could not comprehend nor accredit such barbarity, and some of the most notable blunders have involved innocent and naive visitors from far more advanced physical worlds who cheerfully shared their technology with earthmen.

So there we have the answers to both of our questions — the purpose of the UFO's and their origins. You may now quit reading from the Fount of Wisdom. And once again, I thank you for your help.

WHAT IS THE TRUTH ABOUT SHOWMANSHIP?

If it be argued that vaunting of the ego — the small self — is bad for a given man's progress towards his True Estate, then it must stand to reason that the biggest egotists — performers — are somehow on the road to perdition. Surely they have no chance at redemption or salvation. How can they possibly overcome the small self after having built it up so arduously and for so long a period of time?

Well, the answer is that a great showman — and a showman can be anybody from your pastor or priest or rabbi or mullah, or your homecoming queen, or the U.S. Senator from your state, or an athlete, or the conventional performer on stage or screen be he or she a singer, dancer, actor, musician, comedian, magician, or mime — a great showman is one who derives a natural and powerful high from the energy of his audience. He or she does everything in his or her power to amplify that energy, to bring it to its tilt, to thrill to its surge. And the performer knows that he obtains that energy only to the degree that he enlists the audience's support to his cause. And so he acquires great virtuosity in his skills, to further dazzle and please his audience. Or he rises above himself on those occasions when the stars and his bios are in sync, and gives what is commonly called an "inspired performance". "Inspired" in this context can mean different things, but to many of us it usually means *inspired by God*.

An inspired sermon by your pastor is most assuredly going to be termed an inspiration from God. And it is true. When you appeal to the human beings in an audience for their affections and transfer of energy through them to you, you are showing great love for them. And the more they love you, the more energy you receive from them — you are inspired by this powerful flow of the Cosmic Love Force through them to you, and you transcend your normal technical skills to give a virtuoso performance — an inspired performance.

It is indeed inspired by God. Each member of that audience — no matter how insignificant and humble — is a God. And to have that many Gods on your side, exchanging energy with you during that performance, is to give a God-inspired performance.

Now other creative artists are performers also, even though they are not commonly regarded as such. The writer or composer taps into humanity's common creative pool to deliver exactly those words, exactly those tunes and rhythms and harmonies, exactly those scenes, that the mass of humanity needs to read or hear or see. If a playwright touches the mystical hearts of people as did Thornton Wilder with the play *Our Town*, then it is because those mystical human hearts first projected a need for that theme and words and presentation. Otherwise, Thornton Wilder would not have been able to pull down the final package from Higher Consciousness and present it to us.

When humans, as Gods, want or need something en masse, all the forces of the Cosmos will unite to provide for their need. Divinely Pure Consciousness comes to their aid in this effort and instantaneously it is made known what words or tunes or pictures will prove most useful to that mass of humanity's progress. Divine Consciousness enscribes those words and tunes and pictures in an etheric pool of creativity which all Artists tap and which all artists aspire to tap. It is the highest creative pool. It is Authority in Art. It manifests in no manner whatsoever which is not true and touching to the human heart. It is a Voice you have longed to hear, even though you would never have been able to precisely express your need for It.

It is a Noble Voice that sings only of what is good in Man. It praises Man's spirit and lifts him up, and It tries to get him to recognize himself for what he truly is — a God of the Most High Creation — a fashioner of universes — *A Reflective Counterpart To The Most High Father!*

This Voice will sing endlessly and truly for Man, for It is first and foremost a Voice of Compassion. Because in our recorded history a man called Jesus of Nazareth spoke and taught with this Voice, we have often called the Voice the Christ Voice, but of course many non-Christians have sung and taught with this Voice. There was no nobler embodiment of compassion than Jesus of Nazareth, for he represented a manifestation of the highest spirit ever to suffer mortal coil: the Christ Spirit. When Jesus gave up his soul and psyche and body to this Exalted Spirit, he automatically became an Icon to men, since he was then their Innermost Selves.

Men could not of course then comprehend, and few can now, how they collectively were One Being. Nor could they comprehend the inescapability of their Unity with All That Is, nor could they even comprehend All That Is — Creation.

They saw and still see themselves as separate from one another, with those things labelled "good" which make a man stand out from his fellows. So the most talented individuals among men will most naturally gravitate to the display of those talents to show their assumed superiority.

But then a strange thing happens! The showoff, the vaunter of ego, discovers the energy flow that a sympathetic audience provides. And he feeds on it to such an extent that he reaches ever higher into the Cosmic Talent Pool to deliver the ultimate performance — the inspired performance — a performance truly inspired by God: by us, the audience.

When the performer talks to you, it is really your Higher Self talking to you, telling you what you want and need to hear. When your heart is touched by any performance or work of Art, you know that it is the Voice which has spoken to you. The Christians are correct in naming this Voice the Christ Voice, but you do not have to be a Christian to believe in It, to hear It, or to be ennobled by It. It is the Voice of your Exalted Self, your True Self, the Divine Consciousness. It pulls you to It with the same proportionate strength that you yearn to hear It.

And all men do yearn for It. It is what they search for when they seek Wisdom or wealth or sexual conquest, or fame or power or sainthood. When men wait for...they know not what, they are waiting for a re-uniting with the Divine Consciousness and the constant Song of the Voice.

And when men grow weary of experience and of decay and death, they yearn for their True Estate. They long to rest innocently and purely in the womb of the Holy Mother, to frolic in the endless spiritual springs that surround their Father's mansions. They yearn to sup in the banquet halls of those mansions, and to imbibe the sweet nectar of the Highest Wisdom for dessert. They long to awaken to their true natures, and to assume their True Consciousness. *They pine for home!*

When men are led to transcend their small selves by an inspired performance given by a true showman or Artist, the performer is lifted up to the same degree he has helped lift his audience. Somehow, in the collective energy of the event, when Artist and audience are One, glimpses of the Homeland flash before the eyes of each audience member's heart, and after a sufficient number of such inspirations, performer and audience alike are led to begin in earnest the Homeward Journey — the journey to Self-awakening. Each one will be in search of his True Estate, his long lost Home. But so long as they seek it outside of themselves, they shall never find it.

The door to your Homeland is within you. It is a spark of the Divine Consciousness in your heart, and often It is termed your "heart of hearts". Being multi-dimensional, it manifests on all planes of your being and interpenetrates all of your bodies' hearts, up to and including the Heart of the Celestial Virgin — the Holy Mother — and the Heart of the All Highest Father. You can return home to Unity through the corridor that opens inward from your heart of hearts. You will then remember who you really are, and how it was that you came to be lost in flesh.

You will be awake. And the showman, consciously or unconsciously, will have helped awaken you.

WHAT DO WE MEAN BY "HEART"?

When we say that a work of Art has Wisdom and Truth in it, we do not usually have to explain ourselves further to our audience. There is a common bond of understanding among most men Spirits as to the precise meaning of these words. Even those people who do not know the definitions of these words — either their true definitions or their false definitions — still know the *meaning* of these words because almost all of us are exposed to Truth and Wisdom quite frequently in our normal American lives. These virtues can and do show up even in TV commercials. Whenever creativity is in practice, Truth and Wisdom will often pop up because truly creative people — true Artists — will find that their output, no matter what field of Art and Beauty they trade in, is greatly enhanced if they can somehow endow it with whatever Truth and Wisdom they have at their store. They find that poor works, mediocre works, and even excelling works are made better by seasoning them with Truth and Wisdom. When poeple refer to a piece of Art as a *tour de force*, they are usually implying it displays outstanding craftsmanship but little Truth or Wisdom.

People also apply the *tour de force* appelation to a work of Art that has no *heart*.

We all know what we mean when we say a work of Art has "heart". As with Truth and Wisdom, there is a common Spiritual bonding within our human understanding to instinctively know the meaning of the word in this context. This is true even though few people can provide a definition of *heart*, as when we say a movie has heart, a song or book has heart, or a performance has heart. What is this quality of Artwork that we choose to identify with the heart organ as opposed to the kidneys or lungs or brain? Why, for example, do we not say "that movie had liver"?

The Artwork which has heart is that which touches us in the area of the heart chakra, a chakra so named because of its proximity to our physical body's heart. When something touches us there, we feel a twanging in our breast, immediately adjacent to and sometimes directly over our physical heart. This is not a physical feeling, however. No feeling, even of physical pain, is a physical feeling. Unbeknownst to most men, feeling is not a *sense* as is sight or hearing or smell or taste. Feeling is an integral part of a human being; it is his or her *female* self! When a human being attaches his essence to a physical body, the feeling half of him resides in the nervous system and facilitates the ability to feel hot or cold or pain or pleasure. Man misidentifies this phenomenon as a sense similar to sight or smell. The other half of a human being, the male half, is most properly called *desire* but is also termed *will*, in the sense of a personal will. This half attaches itself to the circulatory system of the physical body, and is thus closely identified with blood.

So a *feeling* is a very integral part of us, as compared to a mere sensation from a mere servant, such as a sense. This is specially true for feelings generated by non-physical stimulation. And this is why "hurt feelings" are always more painful even than intense physical pain. The wounds to our feelings are also much slower to heal than physical wounds. We humans may be extremely careless and foolish when it comes to risking physical pain and physical wounds, as we do when we drive drunk or join the police force or take up hangliding, but we are *extremely* careful and cautious in avoiding wounded feelings.

The "loss of face" which is so feared by our Oriental brethren is naught but a manifestation of hurt feelings. Hurt feelings are more responsible for acts of rage and empires of mayhem than any other motive known to Man. Historians will never find what made Adolf Hitler the demon that he became, for they will never seek the true cause: *hurt feelings*. Somewhere in Adolf's early life, some Jewish person or perhaps a group of Jews unconsciously or perhaps deliberately wounded Adolf Hitler's feelings. Deeply. And it might be found that the act may indeed have been deliberate, and this combined with the fact that it probably occurred during the extremely painful and sensitive teenage years might have served to make the wound a most excruciating one.

It is interesting to wonder if the Divine Intelligence has since made aware the magnitude of their actions to those thoughtless children who taunted Adolf. Hopefully not! They were probably just being normal unfeeling kids, perhaps poking fun at a local nerd. But what horror was reaped from those foolishly-sown seeds!

Feelings are of paramount importance to a person because they are an integral half of a person's being. It matters not if feelings' wounds stem from a man's devotion to his false self. The wounds are nonetheless real because he has permitted them to be, and they have touched a core element within him.

So when our feelings are touched in a positive or friendly way, we are proportionately more pleasured than when we are physically gratified by food, drink, sex, or whatever. A loving pat on our feelings is far more cherished and has much greater impact on us than a loving pat on the fanny. It stands to reason that if hurt feelings are the worst thing a person can endure, then *caressed feelings* or *lifted feelings* can be among the best things a person can enjoy.

We relish having our feelings *lifted up* by a movie that has *heart*. *Heart* in any work of Art is that quality which lovingly touches our feelings, either lifting them up or caressing them gently. A work of Art can also show heart by *enlightening us*. This enlightenment can be intellectual or it can be what is falsely termed emotional — an enlightenment of our feelings. When a work of Art *exercises* our feelings, it enlightens them. In this manner, even sad or tragic themes can inspire a play or movie or novel that is yet "uplifting". Or even paintings of so-called "ugly" objects, such as those rendered by Ivan Albright, can be hauntingly beautiful for their *heart*, their assault on our *feelings*.

Now in the final analysis, when we talk about the Truth, the Wisdom, and the heart of an Artwork, we are in reality talking about *heart* only. For as it turns out, any Wisdom or Truth in a work of Art is going to impact our *feelings*, since Truth in Art is the spiritual Truth of a matter and Wisdom is the spiritual interpretation of that Truth. When we are confronted with what we recognize to be Wisdom, we are *spiritually touched*, and this touch is felt in our *feelings*. So for all intents and purposes, to say a work of Art has Wisdom or Truth is to say it has *heart*, and vice versa.

The degree of Beauty — true Beauty — that an Artwork has is directly proportional to the heart it contains. An Artwork can have a surface beauty, a beauty of form or execution, and still not be a Beautiful work of Art. Again, a *tour de force* usually bears mostly surface beauty, although almost every work of Art has *some* heart to it if it was produced by a human or a group of humans. But those Artworks which are most Beautiful are those which show Wisdom by extolling the Human Spirit or Love or God or Consciousness in any form, or by linking a human being to his Greater Self by affirming his worth, his lovability, and his eternal validity. Or perhaps by simply saying in an ingenious, clever, and artistic way: "You and All That Is are One!".

This is what prouces Beautiful Art. This is what we call *heart*. It is the doorstep to our beautiful female half, our spiritual half: our *feelings*.

IS ENFORCED VIRTUE WISE?

Should enlightened men attempt to prevent unenlightened men from committing unwise and immoral acts?

For example, assume that the countries stocked mainly by the European races were to suddenly evolve to the point where they saw the stupidity and absolute unlawfulness inherent in the act of killing their fellow man — whether through greed or honor or vengeance or "justified warfare". And then, being full aware of the vulgarity and barbarity which surrounds the act of manslaughter in any form, assume that the European countries began to look aghast at the civil and other wars raging in Africa and the Middle East and Asia and South America, and decide that they must intervene to prevent all further bloodshed on Earth.

A debate might then arise among seekers of the Highest Wisdom, to wit: no one has intervened in the past in the Europeans' free will for self-destruction. If men somewhere are still prone to commit murder of their own kind, they will eventually have to work it out of their systems and evolve to the point where they, too, see the vulgarity and insanity of such acts. Therefore, why not let them continue their barbaric practices unmolested?

The other side to the debate would argue: to save a starving man is to interfere with his free will to die of natural starvation, is it not? And yet who among us would not feed a starving man? We have been graced with the Wisdom to see the folly of war, and that same Wisdom requires that we innoculate all populaces against the possibility of warfare just as we would innoculate them against smallpox or diptheria.

The truth of the debate may be hard to determine, since there is ample evidence that we of Earth have been monitored over many centuries by beings of superior morals and superior technology — beings sometimes mislabelled "angels" because of their proclivity for giving instructions to Man in God's name. And there is even more ample evidence to the effect that this monitoring, since the late forties at least, has been growing more intensive. And yet these beings have done nothing to interdict Man's barbarity to his own species, even though they obviously have the ability to enforce any command they might care to give us.

The party line within the UFO literature as to why this is so, is that free will is the most sacred thing in the Cosmos, and that the commandment has gone forth from the Highest Hierarchy: do nothing to abrogate the free will of a free-willed creature anywhere at any time! And so, ever since the famous episode with Moses and the Israelites, which may have indeed been authorized by Man's ruling hierarchy, the UFO crowd has been intervening in low-keyed and instructional ways: through prophets and great literary works such as the Koran, and through lesser communications and even, according to some sources, to the extent of inhabiting human bodies from birth so as to implant a fifth column of leaders among ordinary earthlings who will rise to the occasion when the time is ripe to launch a revolution in consciousness and morals and spirituality among men.

This is exactly what is happening; the foregoing sentence about our friends in the UFO's is not speculation or fancy. It is fact. They are indeed on a mission similar to the mission that the suddenly-enlightened Europeans might make to their more barbarian brothers. They are going to help us raise our consciousness, our morals, and our spirituality. They are doing it without interfering with our free will or impeding the working out of Karmic forces. Being creatures of much greater Wisdom than we, they are doing it in sync with the Silver Express, in concordance with the Divine Will, the Will for the All Highest Good.

It would be easy for an impatient earthling to ask: "Why don't they just get our attention with a few potent displays of power, and then tell us how we should best act and think for our own good and progress?" The reasoning being that if they are our superiors in morals and Wisdom, why should they not then share it with us and enable us to attain to their level of development? The fallacy is that Man does not really want the Wisdom — he wants the power. He wants the technology. Most likely if he were to get it, Man's leaders would see to it that it was put to immediate use in warfare or other acts against his fellow man.

And so the UFO crowd walks a delicate tightrope. The Wisdom they might so gladly share with us also brings Power. Man would accept the Wisdom, but only to get at the Power. Man must first experience a change of heart, and achieve a moral and spiritual transformation, before he can be given the Highest Wisdom. He must rid his heart and soul of murder, lust, greed, and antipathy. He must become aware of the Unity underlying All That Is.

If any one man among men can achieve this awareness — and all men are capable of it — then such a man would find a host of material and spiritual beings stumbling over each other to get to him with gifts of Wisdom. The treasures that would be spread at his feet would be of awesome proportions.

For such a man would be capable of wielding the Wisdom with Wisdom.

IS IT EVIL FOR MAN TO VAUNT
HIS SMALL SELF?

If Unity is the Highest Truth, and if Man's realization of this Truth and of Unity being his True Self is one of Man's most potent realizations, does it then follow that any man who vaunts his false self — who "goes on an ego trip" — is doing something wrong?

Not necessarily! Although total selflessness and total lack of vanity — somewhat akin to what Jesus of Nazareth displayed — might be the most noble virtues Man can possess, this does not mean there cannot be valid arenas of experiencing which might hasten Man toward that enlightened state free of ego, free of vanity. And the chances are, that some of those arenas just might force a soul to pit itself and its talents for living against those of a fellow soul. And both souls can be ennobled by the struggle, no matter who is the loser or winner. And after many such struggles, they both will play each role many times before coming to the realization that both loser and winner are One. The competitive arena is like a big stick, with a losing end and a winning end. He who oft appears to lose may turn out to be the ultimate victor. Thus each end of the stick — the "struggle stick" — is a bipolar end: both negative and positive, victor and vanquished. It is only one's angle of perception that will make one end look like a big "W" and the other end look like a little "L".

When Man comes to realize that the energy poles of the struggle stick are both one, by virtue of their stick creation, and that the stick and millions of others just like it were naught but energy patterns — Ideas — *just like the poles*, then Man's need for competition shall have come to an end. In the meantime, it greatly advances Man's cause to have him pit himself against the elements or his fellow men in some great struggle to see who is the smartest, the strongest, the meanest. Both he and his opponents will profit from the experience, for *experience* is what hones Man's spirit.

Some may say that such struggles, born of ambition or pride or great vanity, are evil. They say this because Man labels "evil" everything he subconsciously knows to be a cause of pain. Nothing is evil unless it causes its perpetrator or his victim, or both, to *suffer*. In the Abstract Universe, there is no evil except the act of knowingly thwarting the Divine Will for the All Highest Good. So long as Man does not do that, his acts are not evil.

So in and of itself, an act of competition is not evil since not only is neither side hurt by the stuggle but both actually profit from it. And therefore a certain pride and self-respect on a winner's part for having emerged triumphant is also not evil; no one is harmed by the act, not even the perpetrator. What *is* evil is the sense of separateness which each opponent must adopt to create suitable conditions for a conflict. If retained beyond and between struggles — and it invariably is — this sense of separateness will definitely bring a man pain, and will continue to do so until he abandons it.

It is a commonly acknowledged fact of earthlife that "we learn by suffering". People do not always specify what they think it is that we learn, but the phrase is widely believed because people can observe that the most noble souls among them seem to be those who have suffered the most. The callous, the hostile, the moral ciphers — all these are obviously and beyond doubt men and women who have not yet suffered. The trusting, the forgiving, the helpful — these are the men and women who have suffered. Suffering teaches men compassion. Suffering eventually forces Man to look to his Innermost Self for guidance and relief, and there he finds — Unity!

So suffering, which springs from "evil", can and does do Man good. Thus in the purest abstract, there is no evil as Man refers to evil. It is all a figment of Man's imaginative world, the dream world where he imagines himself pitted against Creation. Outside of Man's little sphere of consciousness, evil and good are valid universal concepts. But quite simply, they translate only into two phrases: *good* is that which advances the Evolutionary Spiral, and *evil* is that which impedes it.

And since both types of actions, good and evil, are concepts of the Infinite Creator, conceived as part of an arena created for spirits to advance by experiencing such concepts, we are back to the original and Highest Truth of the matter: there is no evil! All That Is, is Good. Evil, like death, is an impossibility to Divine Consciousness at Its highest level, the level of Unity. All That It enfolds is Good, and It enfolds All That Is.

So the best answer to the question: Is it evil for Man to vaunt his small self? is *NO!* Nothing is evil unless thinking so describes it. And vaunting the small self is evil only if you deem to be evil those acts which bring suffering.

HOW TO "PRAY WITHOUT CEASING"

When you *think*, you are using the Substance of Divine Mind — the same Substance which has wrought the Universe and which sustains it on a day-to-day basis — the same Substance which manifests as the Highest Ideals, the Highest Wisdom, the Highest Beauty. You employ a Substance of great potency when you undertake to think a thought or to allow others' thoughts entree to your mind. In fact, this Substance is not only potent, it is Most Holy. It is Consciousness — All That Is — the Divine Father, the Most Holy Virgin Mother, and *you*. It manifests in you by virtue of your small self — your ego, your earthly identity — since your personal self is only an *Idea*. It also manifests in you by virtue of your True Self, which is also an Idea. The Idea behind your True Self is that of a God who loses himself in mortality and falls asleep, and dreams a dream of separateness, and reaps the pain and suffering for misdeeds committed in ignorance of the true nature of the Visible Universe: a unitary, vast playpen for Holy Consciousness to test Its capabilities in.

If Man did not suffer concepts of separateness, he would realize that he is One with the Divine Mind Which Stands Behind All Things. He would realize that Its Substance is all that he has. It gives him self-consciousness, It enables him to intellectualize, to feel pleasure, to feel pain, and to perceive Creative Projections of Consciousness as Reality. In addition, It moulds the atoms of his physical being, and directs the atoms in the moulding of molecules, and the molecules in the moulding of cells, and the cells in the moulding of organs. Divine Ingenuity stands behind Man's human machine, and such machines are nearly indestructible when men do not consciously interfere with their operation.

In addition to being the Stuff of your consciousness and the Stuff of your body's form and consciousness, Divine Mind is the Creator and Sustainer of all that you see in the visible universe. In short, Consciousness — the Divine Mind — is the heart and soul of everything we are capable of experiencing or knowing. It is the *true* Holy Spirit, for It is quite simply All That Is.

So when we misuse this Substance called Mind for daydreaming, passing judgment on others, or fostering negative emotions, we are indeed committing blasphemy of a most high order. Although Divine Mind created the concepts of *emotions* and *feelings*, and derived the ingenious effects that these things have upon Man and his perception of Reality, we usually do not in earthly language ever imply that Mind or Mindstuff is associated in any way with emotions or feelings. But It is, and not just because Divine Mind created these phenomena. It is also because we men use our Mindstuff to actually *generate* emotions and feelings. These aspects of Man can and do exist independently of intellect or any exercise thereof, yet they are most commonly formed by, and intensified by, our thoughts. Man can and does misuse the Divine Mindstuff to think thoughts of resentment, for example, leading to feelings of anger and the emotion of hate. Man also uses the Divine Mindstuff to curse other people or things, to think despairing thoughts, to worry about events that will not come to pass, and in general to create discordant vibrations in the unitary web of Mindstuff.

For be assured, it is a solitary Organism, this Thing called Consciousness. It is the only Thing that is, that ever was, or ever will be. All other things spring from Its creation. It is the Supreme God. And It is your very essence, the Source and Sustainer of your existence, *the only thing you truly possess or can ever possess!*

When the impact of these High Truths truly hits us, it is easy to feel most ashamed for all of our past misguided and petty thoughts. But there is no value in brooding over them; the value in our remorse stems from the inevitable change in our attitude. If we truly realize that how we use our share of the Divine Mindstuff has an effect, good or bad, on the total organism and on everything within It, we feel an urge to terminate negative or useless thoughts and to devote our mental energy only to positive thoughts, and to thoughts seeking Wisdom. We begin to flood our thinking with thoughts of appreciation for the Divine Beauty which surrounds us. We fervently strive to remain in harmony with the Divine Will, and to use our Mindstuff only to advance our roles as agents of that Will. Such is the power of realizing — truly realizing — that there is only One.

There are many people who realize this most vital Law not consciously, but subconsciously or superconsciously. These people almost always become Science of Mind or Power of Thought subscribers or advocates. They intuitively know that Mindstuff is all powerful, and that Its power can be properly exploited by Man to his greater benefit.

But positive thinking advocates do not always realize that positive thinking alone will not preserve them from all harm. For example, it most certainly cannot forestall the demise of the physical body and of its ego, the small self. And yet oddly enough, true believers in the fact that it *can* do such things will be led to a method whereby they can bypass the experiencing of the demise of their physical organisms — actually "escape death" — so that it could be said that yes, positive thinking can indeed charm away death. And yet it will not, unless its practitioners also become practitioners of the mode of thinking prescribed to circumvent the need for the death experience.

Death can be bypassed for this earthly life, and for all future earthly lives if any, by voluntarily surrendering the small self's existence well before it can be torn asunder and overcome by the Higher Self at time of bodily death. The attitude should be: my ego is going to go away anyway — it is only a temporary mad dream — it cannot possibly endure — therefore why not give it up *now?*. What further sense is there in keeping my Self attached to it for another 20, 30, or at the most, 60 years?

Give the small self, the ego, no more power. Funnel no intellectual energy to it. Divorce and detach yourself from it. Subjugate it, humble it. It is your most insidious and deadly enemy. In fact, *it is the only enemy you have!*

Consecrate your personal will to the Will of the All Highest Father. Pray feverishly that this merging of wills be brought to pass in all that you think and do and experience. Take no thought unto your small self, but instead "in all things give thanks".

Devote your allotment of the Divine Mindstuff to a quest for *more*, for a greater allotment. Use your mental energy to seek out the Highest Wisdom of all matters. Replace daydreams with ponderings over the magnificent Unity of All Things, over the absolute inseparability of you from the Divine Mind, and of the fact of Consciousness being the only *thing* in All Things.

This is truly "praying without ceasing", this giving up of the ego. Praying without ceasing is seeking to know the earthly Truth and the Spiritual Truth — the Wisdom — of All Things. It is also the pursuit of the Highest Ideals, the Highest Art, the Highest Beauty. Praying without ceasing is looking up toward your True Self, not down at your false self. After prolonged practice of praying without ceasing, the small self withers for want of attention and energy, and dies an unnoticed death.

When the small self thus perishes from lack of your Mindstuff's energy, you are freed of the experience known as "death". You realize that death was a "necessity" all of these years only because we are consumed with the *illusion* that it is. It was the only way in which Man could conceive of being freed from the tyranny of his ego and the insane nightmares it constantly produces. Your constant praying — your positive and uplifting thoughts, your gratitude to Creation for All That Is and for All Experience — your gratitude to the All Highest Father for the Stuff of Consciousness and for your very existence — your love of Wisdom and its counselled behavior — your love of your True Self, the Living Christ — all of this constitutes "praying without ceasing", and it will *set you free!*

You will literally be able to transform and transpose your physical body and its consciousness to a higher dimension, either at the time of physical death or when physical death is impending, or even well before physical death is destined to occur. You will, when this happens, be a Christed One — one who is possessed of Cosmic Consciousness, one who is in tune with the All. And like the Christed Jesus of Nazareth, you could be crucified even unto death yet still resurrect and revitalize your physical organism to perfect health and form were there a need to do so!

Thus the Christian dogma about Christ being your savior; more accurately it is Christ Consciousness which is your savior, and not the sacrifice of the body of the Christed Jesus. No one can die for you, nor save you from your sins, nor even forgive your sins, other than *you.* The burden of performance, of attitude, and of thought — your usage of the Divine Mind — is upon you and you alone.

But after you have taken the first step, after your heart has willed this change in you to come about, then will you have a most potent helper and advisor and guide steering you along the right paths at all times: your High Self, your True Self — the *Living Christ.*

HOW DO YOU ACTUALLY "GIVE UP THE EGO"?

Well, it would help if you were one of us nerds because, unless you are some kind of spiritual genius, you will almost certainly have to shun all but the most superficial human contact — all of it. This is because learning how to "pray without ceasing" can be an extremely difficult task if there is close contact with any human who is not on the same path, who does not share your goals. Any such close contact will, in fact, almost ensure your failure. While learning how and practicing to pray without ceasing, the faintest negative vibration from a fellow human of any intimacy can be akin to a red-hot nail driven into your emotional body. Your emotions become stretched to the breaking point by the agony of such occurrences and you begin to find that the least little event sets you off in a rage or frenzy or into some other such negative release of emotional energy. To prevent this chain of events, you automatically give up trying to shed the ego and you join the negative chorus of human thought to immunize yourself against the pain that comes from the common pool of negativity.

All this does not mean you have to become a hermit, however — you can even live in a city, although a small town or the countryside would be much preferred. And wherever you live, it would help if there is a great deal of natural beauty nearby, to make it easier for you to confront Beauty and to praise Its gifts to Man, and to thank the All Highest Father for the very Concept of Beauty, and for the profound pleasure it can bring a hungry soul — a soul starving for Truth and Wisdom and Justice and unification of will with the Will for the All Highest Good.

You will also be forced to shun the popular culture. The only TV programs which you will be able to endure will be news and sports and documentaries. But should any truly uplifting drama be available, or should any form of high comedy present itself for your entertainment, you could definitely avail yourself of these vehicles should they suit your taste.

Humor, joy, and good, high spirits are immense aids to the mental discipline necessary for praying without ceasing. Labor of any sort is taboo, unless it be in isolated surroundings. The labor itself can be most beneficial to your efforts, but co-workers in most jobs, even on an impersonalized factory assembly line, would constitute close human contact by virtue of the daily longevity of the contact.

In short, it would appear that those people in our society who are best positioned to awaken themselves through ego sacrifice are winos, other street people, disabled workers and shut-ins, lighthouse keepers, solitary night watchmen, and other such isolated jobholders, and retired people in single status. If you have a spouse, and if you cannot get him or her to go along with you on yhour quest, you must separate yourself from that spouse or else forego your own attempt. "And every one that hath forsaken houses, or brethren, or sisters, or father, or mother, or wife, or children, or lands, for my name's sake, shall receive an hundredfold, and shall inherit everlasting life. But many that are first shall be last; and the last shall be first."

No one ever said that giving up the ego is easy. In fact, it is the ego itself that makes it so difficult. It is the ego which says "I'm not going to leave my family and friends and go off without a job or any means of support just so I can learn to pray without ceasing". The ego derives part of its identity from its fellow egos, and it pays identity homage to them in return, and it does not in any manner cherish the thought of losing this vital exchange. If it loses that, it just may lose its *owner's* beliefs in its good looks or its charm or its suavity or its intellect. And then it will have lost control altogether!

This importance of other egos to an ego cannot be overstated. The mutual web of articificiality and posing which they collectively spin constitutes but one of the many nets over Man's True Self, yet when he has rent all of the other nets, this one proves the toughest to tear himself away from: friends, acquaintances, relatives. His social contacts help him form his identity even as he does theirs. Yet oddly enough, the human's herding instincts are such that if two or three members of any social group were to go off in quest of ego-sacrifice, the chances are that more than a few of their compatriots would pick up the baton and follow!

But, sad as it may be to leave your past behind in order to set off in search of freedom, you should remember that there is, as always, a happy ending to the story. You see, he or she who *succeeds* in sacrificing the ego can return to his or her social enclave a much-improved being — a shining beacon of the glory of self-sacrifice — and this beacon illuminates the sterling example which the achiever truly is to humanity at large, and not just to his or her immediate social group.

In fact, the successful achievers, if they so desire it, can actually enlarge their social mileau to any extent they may desire, once they have successfully aligned themselves with the All Highest Father's Will. If they be people who relish and need and flourish with human social contact, they will be put to use among men in roles involving heavy doses of such contact. But beyond social intercourse, the first and foremost functions of these achievers will be, as with all other achievers, the extolling of the Divine One's main Virtue: *Unity*. They will pronounce to all whom they enounter: separateness is a deadly illusion, we are all of one Stuff! We have the same Mother and the same Father; we are *siblings!* We are as inseparable from each other as each of us is from his High Self! We are *One!*

This, dear reader, is the Ultimate Social Life. You need give up *nothing* of substance in order to undertake the ego-killing quest. You can beat death — you truly can. The desire must be yours. The commitment must be yours. *The first step must be yours.*

THE ABSOLUTE NECESSITY OF FOLLOWING CHRISTIAN TEACHINGS

One literally can have no idea of the powerful position in the Cosmos held by Men spirits. Man is literally a God among the Universal Order of Entities. Even those things whom Man believes to be his masters — such as nature, other men, his personal ego, his body — even they are most subservient to him once he accepts the Truth about himself. He is commonly regarded as a majestic being by all Universal Personalities.

Therefore does the mere act of a man pointing himself upward, yearning for the Highest Wisdom, longing for an awareness of his Unity with All That Is — the Eternal Father — therefore does this mere act by a man set forth a marshalling of Universal Forces to the satisfaction of that yearning. Everything material and spiritual will bend itself to the attainment of such a yearning, for all Forces rejoice when a Man spirit, a veritable sleeping God, stirs toward an awakening. These Forces will see to it most assuredly that the Wisdom which a man seeks is made available to him. If his motives be pure, if he truly seeks to know who he is and to come awake, a man cannot fail in obtaining his heartfelt desire. Awesome Forces are at his disposal. He can wield Wisdom like a scythe that cuts down the shallow, the false, the rigid, the immature. He *thinks* in his heart, he *feels* in his heart, and he *loves* in his heart. His heart is big, and soft, and mellow. He is a teddy bear, a pussycat, an indulgent, patient mother. He judges no one and no thing, but always seeks the rightness or wrongness of a matter in his heart. If the flame flickers, it is wrong: the answer is negative. If the flame burns steady, it is right: the answer is positive.

The man awakens, and returns to his true Immortal Estate, and never again knows death. Such is what the mere desire, the mere longing, the mere heartfelt love for Truth and Wisdom and Unity can bring! Because, once a role appeals to a man, he finds that *the mere acting of that role places him in the role!* This is the magic of the teaching given us by Jesus of Nazareth when he spoke in the Bible with the Christ Voice, and when he continues to speak to us in this Voice.

Assume that a man sues another man at law. Man 'A' asks damages of man 'B' for libel, let us say. Man 'B' says: "Take what you will; all that I have is yours for the asking anyway, for we are truly one. You need not engage a lawyer, nor secure a court's judgment, nor need you even bear me a legitimate grievance. If I have something you want or need, ask for it: it is as much rightfully yours as it is mine."

Were someone in man 'B's position to respond to such an attack in such a manner, it would most assuredly not be through mere foolishness. Such a response would and could extend only from the Highest Wisdom. 'B' would do so because he knew that no man anywhere really *owns* anything — all that he has is merely on loan from Creation. It matters not whether he came by his possessions honorably or dishonorably; quite simply, they are not really his to keep nor to give away. So long as he does not give to foster weakness in his fellow man, he is obligated to give whatever is requested of him.

Now it could happen that such a man as man 'B' might have no possessions at all once his attitude became well known, for the truly needy — whether deserving of his largesse or not — will strip him bare. But such a man as man 'B' will also *never go in want of any material thing*, for there will be more of his fellows willing to *give* than there are those who are willing to *take!*

And as for the lawsuit: well, man 'A' would of necessity terminate his legal action and all claims against 'B', feeling it impossible to attack one who puts up no defense, and who feels about him the way 'B' does. For the first time in his life, 'A' would see, truly see firsthand, how turning the other cheek is the best course of reaction to hostility at all times. It displays Unity. In fact, it is the only possible reaction to hostility that a belief in Unity can counsel. "Love your enemies, bless them that curse you, do good to them that hate you, and pray for them which despitefully use you, and persecute you." "And if any man will sue thee at the law, and take away thy coat, let him have thy cloke also."

It is a most unearthly way to behave. And therein lies its power and its Wisdom, for in a civilization as backward as ours, unearthly behavior is often the most proper behavior. Unearthly behavior constitutes the opposite of manslaughter, the opposite of fear, the opposite of antipathy and phoniness and sickness and decay and death. Unearthly behavior is *spiritual* behavior, where one is aware of the One Spirit and one's inseparability from It, and of Its inclusiveness of All Things.

And the amazing fact is, *that this is Man's normal mode of behavior!* This is the way Man is supposed to be, the way he behaves in his True Estate, and therefore the way he can behave if so convinced of its Wisdom. The Christian Mystery *told* us and *showed* us how an Enlightened One is supposed to act, and all a man need do is to don the role and presto! he *becomes* the role. It is an incredibly easy way to resurrect oneself from the living dead of Earth, from the ranks of sleepwalkers who refer to themselves as the "living".

Poverty, chastity, and non-attachment to earthly or material things was the Idea counselled by the Passion Play. There is no way to escape it: if you want out of the endless round of death, decay, and suffering, if you are tired of staying in the same primitive, unaware condition all the time, if you truly seek Wisdom, then you have no alternative but to obey to the letter the teachings and examples of Jesus of Nazareth. It is that simple; that cut-and-dried. No matter how foolish or impractical it may seem to you, that is what it takes to be saved. And that is why Christians always refer to Christ as their Savior, even when they are not yet of a mind to follow His advice.

But the True Christ — not Jesus of Nazareth, but the True Living Christ — would have it made known that His patience is infinite, as infinite as his love for you, and as faithful about your return to Him as you are faithless in the execution of His counselled behavior and beliefs. For He would have it also made known that you and He are truly One, no matter how much you may deny that fact or even deny Him as a Person — the Person that is your most True Self. He would have you think of this every waking moment of your day, along with the fact that through Him you are united with All That Is. When this then becomes such a habit with you that you can do other things, think other thoughts, while still remembering your Unity with God, through Christ, then shall you also be awake.

As the mighty creations that we, as men, are, we are obligated to eventually emulate the Christed behavior of Jesus of Nazareth. There is really no escaping it. True, we might choose to tarry another 30 or 40 or 500 lifetimes on Earth, especially if we find suffering to be enjoyable, but eventually we will have to go along with the crowd. It all hinges, I suppose, on when we become tired, truly *weary*, of the endless cycle of birth, decay, and death, and of the delusion, and of the deceit, and of the barbaric cruelty of Man towards Man. It hinges on when we get tired of the *game*, and begin longing for Reality. It hinges, I suppose, on when we become truly, heartachingly *homesick*.

For it will be then that we begin our journey home.

THE ILLUSION CALLED "FEAR"

Men have attempted to define fear either as an emotion or as a state of mind. It is neither. It is an illusion, and it is perhaps the most prevalent, common, and damaging illusion under which we mortals suffer.

The term *fear* in this context does not by any means refer to that state of body-consciousness which the physical organism feels when its existence is threatened, and the adrenalin flows, and fight or flight decisions are contemplated. That is "fear", but only because we have no other word for it. It is a mechanical fear, an unconscious fear. We should find a suitable synonym for such fear since although it can be conquered by wiser and cooler heads it is nonetheless a beneficial feature of our physical organism.

The *true* fear, the fear which does so much damage to Man's psyche, soul, and body, stems solely from Man's ignorance; from his self-imposed limited supply of True Consciousness. It is an illusion born of the misuse of what paltry stores of Consciousness a man does possess. It is, if you examine it from a distant, detached state of mind, a highly comical thing. Here is this poor under-endowed conscious entity called "Man" who is aware enough and alert enough to recognize that he is indeed "mortal", that disasters can and do occur which shorten his mortality, and that beyond mortality lies heaven-knows-what wherein no doubt greater and even more painful disasters probably lurk awaiting his discovery. Yet on the other hand, this shortsighted creature does not possess sufficient consciousness or awareness to realize just *who* he really is, or that he is truly *invincible* and that his fear serves only one purpose: to bring disaster down upon his shoulders.

After the following two sentences are read, many "but what about..." questions will spring into readers' minds. THERE IS NOTHING ANYWHERE IN THE COSMOS, ON ANY PLANE OF BEING, WHICH IS CAPABLE OF CAUSING YOU TRUE HARM! There is nothing anywhere at any time which merits even one dash of that illusion called fear.

"But what about muggers and rapists?" "But what about cancer?" "But what about black magicians?" So go the objections to the Highest Truth of the matter, the Truth that you have absolutely nothing to be afraid of at any time. Man's mind is capable of such negative use of the Divine Stuff of Consciousness that he will concoct endlessly a series of "real" things that can harm him and which pose a potential threat to his well-being. *But it is all an illusion,* just like so many other things pertinent to our sad state of existence. The Reality, the Eternal Reality, is this: that you are an impregnable fortress of Spirit, and that nothing can penetrate that fortress to your disadvantage except that you allow it. *You,* and you alone, are the only thing worth fearing. It is only you who can bring harm to yourself. And it is only through your succumbing to the illusion called fear that you can bring about such harm.

"Accidents" do not "happen". They stem from past thoughts on your part which, due to your Godhood, have set Universal Forces into action to bring about a reality consistent with your thoughts and expectations. If you deem yourself a guilty, condemnable creature for some act you have committed in response to your thoughts, you may subconsciously or superconsciously generate an event which will painfully bring home to you the lack of wisdom behind such thoughts and acts. If you instead *fear* retribution for your thoughts and acts, you in effect do the same thing. The offsprings of Consciousness, which is All That Is, are highly sensitive to the expectations of any form of Consciousness, even that misguided and self-limited form which you employ daily. These offsprings — the ether, materiality, other entities — Creation Itself — are like clay ready for your moulding. There will always be a criminal seeking a victim; if you fear victimization either because you deserve it or because you just happen to like indulging the illusion of fear, you may find that Creation responds to this negative use of Precious Mindstuff in a rather detached manner: you become the criminal's victim.

This basic Truth, should you elect to sbuscribe to it, does not give you the right to "flaunt fate". That is, should you come to realize that truly there is nothing worthy of your fear, you should not necessarily attempt to cross expressways in the middle of the day, or to walk crime-ridden sections of your cities in the middle of the night. On the other hand, should circumstances so occur as to put you into a position where you absolutely *must* do such things, then you may do so with impunity and with absolute fearlessness. THERE IS SIMPLY NO WAY IN WHICH YOU WILL BE HARMED!

Whatever paths the Will for the All Highest good may lead you down will be safe paths, for this is the Law. Only you can render those paths dangerous or harmful. You do this by the illusion of fear, which is born of distrust, self-centeredness, enmity, and ignorance. If you cease to ignore the Holy Truth of Unity, you will find yourself shorn of distrust, self-centeredness, and enmity, and fear shall no longer be your constant companion.

The most prevalent fear among men is the fear of "death". Consequently, the most fervent objection to the Basic Truth we are now considering runs along these lines: we are mortal, and therefore "death" is a certainty to us, so how can we say we need have no fear? Something somewhere and some time will bring an end to this physical body of ours. Is it not foolish to not fear it? The answer to this objection is that men have always had, and will always have, a fear of the unknown. Because in our self-imposed state of ignorance the phenomenon we know as "death" — which is yet another illusion — is an uninvestigated and great unknown, we stand in fear of it. Were we to understand it, it could in no wise be regarded with other than eager anticipation, and certainly never with fear, even if we have not conquered the illusion of fear! An anonymous speechwriter for F. D. Roosevelt made a great contribution to the common store of Wisdom when he wrote that we have nothing to fear but fear itself. Truer words were never spoken or written by Man, yet the obviousness of this pithy observation is so straightforward that our perverted minds choose to admire it and then to promptly dismiss it.

Absence of fear can be obtained in the same manner as the absence of any other illusion: through enlightenment. And enlightenment is naught but increasing your allotment of Consciousness and decreasing your allotment of ignorance. Any one of the forementioned methods for increasing your store of Consciousness will result in a concomitant reduction, even to the point of elimination, of fear's grip on your mind. Align your will with the Divine Will. Ask that your cup of Consciousness be increased. Or exploit the Law of Giving by pouring forth your share of the Divine Light Force onto all things or beings that you come in contact with or are otherwise made aware of.

The return on your investment in the form of the elimination of fear is itself a powerful incentive to become more conscious. The freedom which you will find once you have eliminated fear from your life is such that you will give eternal thanks for having read these words. The Seal of the All Highest Father is upon this promise.

ARE BOOZE AND DRUGS
BAD FOR MAN?

In most respects, they are. The worst of the pharmacopia which Man ingests is of course alcohol, not just because it is in such widespread usage but also because of the physiological and psychological havoc it wreaks. Its ability to enslave Man is unique, since it is adept at promoting both chemical dependency and psychological dependency. And its seduction talents are unequalled, since one's first enounters with it are almost always pleasant. Those people who escape alcohol's clutches throughout life are usually those who either had a major, sickening bout of drunkeness on their first encounter with the drug, or those who abstained totally from any first encounter. Those religions which have proclaimed an absolute ban on alcohol have done many of their followers a great favor.

But alcohol's most condemnable trait is its capacity for bringing out the worst nature of some of its users. The family slayings, barroom murders, vicious beatings, and other barbaric acts of blind violence which alcohol promotes constitute the most shameful statistics the Western World has ever ignored. The damages to society caused by alcohol are such that no sane society anywhere can countenance its legality.

And yet — as always — there is another side to the coin. Nothing, it seems, is ever black or white.

If I were sole ruler of this planet, and it were given to me as part of my natural powers to ban alcohol from Earth by edict, I would not do so, even knowing the Higher Wisdom about alcohol's seamier side. The reason is quite simple: for all of its harm it still does enough good to warrant its continued availability. It is, you see, the only fast and easy pain reliever for *psychic* pain that Man possesses.

Those of us who cannot control our own bodies, and we are legion, will ingest aspirin or another pain reliever for a headache or stiff neck or toothache. We could of course eliminate the pain or its cause without drugs through various meditative techniques, but as stated above, those of us who cannot control our bodies need the fast and easy solution.

Similarly, sufferers of grief, remorse, hopelessness, melancholy, and other such psychic pain could easily meditate away the pain and/or its cause, but like us headache sufferers they lack the faith. And what do they have to turn to for a quick and easy palliative besides alcohol? It is an *excellent* painkiller for both psychic and physical pain.

Perhaps this helps explain why teetotalers are often harsh, judgmental, and unempathetic people. Prolonged psychic pain without some form of relief — something to make one step back from oneself and see things in perspective — will undoubtedly lead many people to some form of personality warping and hardening of the heart. This indeed may after all be alcohol's most important service to Man: softening and mellowing the heart of those men who would not otherwise enjoy such a service from any other means, natural or artificial.

Assume that *you* were sole ruler of this planet: could you ban alcohol without an effective substitute for its function as a psychic painkiller and heart mellower? You most probably could not, and so we are stuck with demon booze, at least for the immediate future.

The illegal drug heroin is bad mainly for the chemical dependency it creates, and yet that is also a chief feature of Valium, which of course is legal. The knowing reader might add that this is all due to financial considerations. This is true, and it is true for both drugs. Valium is legal because the vested financial interests of the world profit from its legality, and need to keep it legal. And heroin is illegal because the vested financial interests of the world need *it* to be kept illegal. If you reverse the legal situations for these two drugs, all profits come to a halt and much blood will be spilt.

Otherwise, heroin would be much less harmful to Man than alcohol. The unique illegality of the drug creates an enscripted army of thieves and muggers and burglars who must convert your property into cash for the pockets of the drug traders and their political friends who keep the drug illegal and who promote addiction to it among society's weaker elements. Therefore, a tremendous amount of crime is attributed to heroin addiction, and the "good forces" of society, because of this crime, press for more efforts at suppressing heroin's importation and sale, thereby driving prices higher and creating even more crime! The American Public is truly not noted for its powers of reason.

The "drug" that is an excellent substitute for alcohol as a heart mellower, but not as a killer of psychic pain, is marijuana. This substance has the added advantage of causing no physiological damage to its users, while on the other hand there are several ways in which it is actually physiologically beneficial to Man.

Those artists and writers who slowly destroyed themselves and their talent with alcohol abuse because they could not create in a sober state of mind — that is, they used alcohol to still the small ego enough to put themselves into an alpha state — could have prolonged their careers immensely and even have produced better output had they made use of cannabis instead of booze. If you are of a creative bent, you should try to establish a rapport with marijuana and, in common terminology, "get mellow". It can cause paranoid reactions in some users, so it should never be imbibed unless you are in an unworried, non-apprehensive frame of mind. Marijuana, like alcohol, helps you still the petty, personal self, and to let more of your True Self shine through. If you know people who indulge in this plant, you will almost always observe that they are nicer, friendlier, more empathetic, and more sensitive when they are under its influence than when they are not, just like many drunks you may have known. For alcohol, like marijuana, deadens the sense of small, personal self, and allows a more Unity-oriented Self to control its users, at least up until the time alcohol acquires control of its users and summons their animal, base selves in replacement of the small selves.

If you indulge in the pursuit of High Ideals while under marijuana's influence, such as the appreciation of Beauty or the seeking of Wisdom, you will build up a rapport with the substance which operates along the lines of post-hypnotic suggestion. Once you practice nobility of thought under marijuana you will, with each subsequent submission to its influence, be placed in a frame of mind conducive to further nobility of thought! This is a truly miraculous trait of the substance cannabis, so much so that it is not hard to foresee a religion springing up around this phenomenon in the future. In this peculiar capacity, marijuana serves as an excellent beginning intermediary to the contact of one's High Self.

I do not know why marijuana continues to be illegal, especially when the U. S. Congress commissioned a study into its longterm effects on Man and the study totally exonerated the substance! But if we seek an answer to this enigma, we will probably find it, as always, a matter of mammon. In other words, there are more vested financial interests which stand to lose than there are those which stand to gain from marijuana's legalization, so it will probably continue to be illegal for the foreseeable future.

But as a free spirit, you have a sacred right and a holy duty to break any law that is unnecessary or which exists purely to promote self-centered financial interests against the Will for the All Highest Good. Should you care to judge the goodness or badness of cannabis for yourself, feel free to do so at any time, with no sense of civic or personal guilt whatsoever.

After all, do not all of us drive faster than 55 miles per hour?

WHAT IS THE TRUTH ABOUT SPIRITUALISM?

There does exist in the literature of spiritualistic phenomena quite a bit of incontrovertible evidence attesting to the after "death" survival of human personalities and their occasional ability to communicate with those of us still ensconced in the three-dimensional space/time illusory world.

By no means, however, does this warrant any attempt on the part of any human being to communicate with discarnate entities, no matter how worthy the motive may appear to our limited realms of sense. The reason is this: even when successful, you will seldom contact the true Self or Spirit of the dearly departed, and you will open yourself up to even greater delusions than those you suffer by virtue of your more normal pastimes. Also, in many cases you will cause real harm to the entity you attempt to contact, disrupting its normal progress in weaning itself from our nightmarish world of pain, decay, and death.

In fact, the nightmare analogy is most appropriate here: who among us would, upon awakening a child from a nightmare, induce him to re-live the unpleasantness by questioning him as to its details? Our wisest, and fortunately our most normal course of action, is to prod the child to forget the experience and to assure him that "it was only a dream; it wasn't real; you're o.k. now".

When you attract the attention of a departed earthly personality through mediumistic intervention, you are only encouraging him to hang on to a nightmare which nature insists he forget. Only under the most rare and extraordinary circumstances would you ever be able to converse with that entity's truer self, or to have access to the truer self's fount of wisdom. You will be contacting a soul made no wiser by the mere act of passing over, for this act does little to enlighten our illusory selves. Usually the only immediate wisdom gained is that death is indeed a myth, and that we the "living" are in actuality the dead ones — the living dead. But you can gain this assurance from consulting the ample literature already available on the subject, without disturbing the rightful occupations of the recently departed.

Sometimes spiritualism can be excused in its role of freeing Earthbound entities who were perhaps suicides or victims of a particularly violent or untimely death. But even then you are not communicating with the true entity, but with the astral shell of the entity, an emotionally-charged automaton which nonetheless is capable of holding its truer self in a form of earthly bondage much as a corporeal body in advanced senility can hold its true self in earthly bondage.

On occasion, even the senile can make enough sense to indicate that they are indeed remnants of an earthly personality whom they used to be, but the "sense" is more like a recording on the brain that has been somehow triggered and is now playing itself back randomly, out of context, and for little purpose. Much the same phenomenon can occur when you undertake to converse with the departed: the thing called the astral shell of the entity is contacted and its repository of earthly memories is played back quite convincingly and quite lifelessly to those who may have known the entity during its earthly life. These are truly zombies, and to derive comfort from such communications is the very incarnation of morbidity.

At other times, other earthbound spirits of depraved humor and ill will might animate these astral shells solely for the diversion of communicating with corporeal beings, whose estate they greatly admire. In extreme cases, susceptible earthly communicants and mediums can run the risk of having these earthbound riff-raff attach themselves to the three-dimensionsal world by using the communicants or the medium themselves as a sort of reverse medium. Acts of mayhem and unspeakable crimes can often be attributed to such possessions, especially when perpetrated by otherwise straight, mild-mannered, and harmless individuals.

The bottom line is: do not dabble in spiritualism. Sate your curiosity on the subject with the written results of others' dabbling if you so desire, but have nothing to do with it yourself. There is no Wisdom or knowledge available to you through these means which is not also available to you directly through your own High Self or through the documented searchings and findings of others.

But as to the truth of these and similar matters: scoff not, for there are more things in Heaven and Earth than are dreamt of in your philosophies.

WHAT TRULY IS RELIGION?

First, All That Is — Consciousness — generates Holy Thought, from which human intellect and human thoughts are derived.

Philosophy is the highest exercise of Thought, and Religion is the highest exercise of Philosophy.

Not "religion" in the connotation it holds for Western Man's ears. We are inclined to associate the meaning of the word with a given earthly religion or church, such as the Roman Church or the Anglican Church or the Greek Church. These and all other Western religions are worthy institutions, which have apparently done Man a great deal of good, but they are not truly Religion. When you read below what Religion truly is, you will understand most readily what is meant by this assertion.

Religion says to a man: the Highest Wisdom is your privileged inheritance, so *seek* it! Religion — true Religion — says to a man: you truly have the spark of divinity within you, and it can be fanned into a flame of Godhood only through your own efforts, so *visualize* it! True Religion says to a man: I do not have all the answers, for if I did the Universe of Thought would be a finite One, and we both know It is not. We — you and I — will *never* have all the answers, for there will always be new questions and mystical enigmas to explore in the infinitely-expanding Cosmos. Therefore keep an open mind at all times, *even to arguments contradicting my Truths.* Weigh all issues fairly, without emotion, and trust your heart's mind to decide properly for you what the Truth of a matter is.

(Enscriber's note: The mention of the "heart's mind" by the Higher Wisdom, speaking as Religion, is in reference to one of the most basic and potent occult truths known to men. If you know of this heart mind and respect it, it will guide you far more unerringly than your brain mind ever could. We have been well advised that "as a man thinketh in his heart, so is he". This means that the purest consciousness, the Highest Consciousness, can be obtained more easily through the heart than it can via the brain. They both share the same Stuff of Holy Consciousness, but the flow of this Stuff is far less polluted in the heart mind than it is in the brain mind, providing of course that you are not someone who has hardened your heart over the years.)

True Religion also says to Man: there is no sin, only ignorance. Since all are ignorant in comparison to the next more knowledgable entity on the endless Universal Spiral, you are not to be blamed. But righteous rebuke from the Most High Father's Emissaries of Light will be yours if you strive not to escape your ignorance. For since All are One, you impede All Creation in its evolutionary spiral if you allow yourself to stagnate and do not achieve progress in the lessening of your ignorance. True Religion says that Man is forgiven his sins *even before he commits them,* since there is no sin and therefore nothing to forgive, now or ever.

Religion in Its truest form has only one commandment to Man: "that he should Love, and Love, and Love again." Since Love, the True Love referred to in this quote, is Holy Thought in action — Consciousness going out to know Itself and Its capabilities — it is understood by this commandment that Man should strive to be as conscious as possible on all three levels of his being.

Religion in Its truest form has only one piece of dogma for Its adherents: Unity. It is True Religion's dogma that Man strive to understand the Reality of Unity and to comprehend the awesome ramifications of this most vital Concept. It is True Religion's dogma that Man contains the Cosmos within him, as well as vice versa, and that the infinite evolutionary spiral is therefore *inward* as well as outward. "The Kingdom of Heaven is within you!" And so is All Else, including Religion and Philosophy, and the Most Sacred Christ, and the Divine Father, the Ancient of Days, and the Pure Virgin Mother, Queen of Angels.

True Religion says that knowing these things can lift you up, can awaken you, can restore you to your True Estate.

This is Philosophy in Its highest form. This is Religion.

HOW TO CONQUER SUFFERING

It may thrill you, especially if you are afflicted with chronic anxiety, to know that it is a basic, root Law of the Cosmos that no creature can be allowed to suffer beyond its capacity for endurance. That is, whatever comes your way in the form of suffering will be quite bearable to you. You cannot be given more pain than you are well capable of taking.

Now the nature of our earthlife entails suffering. Suffering, brought on by mistaken behavior that men call "sin", seems to be the only way we have of permanently learning that our wrong behavior is indeed *wrong*. The saintly ones among us — the most empathetic and forgiving and loving humans our species has to offer — seem to always be those who have suffered most. If you cannot find a trace of suffering in their current lives, then consider their prior lives. Unless they are not of the Earth, their virtuous nature would assuredly not have come to be what it is without suffering.

When Man first got lost and trapped in materiality, he was so overwhelmed with the illusion of "substance" and its "separateness" from him that he became blinded to his True Self. But he was a pure creature, not yet knowing lust or vanity or deceit. This pristine untaintedness is the only possible moral state for one who has just entered earthlife. Thus we invariably find it repeated in the children of our species.

The loss of purity that developing humans undergo is at first taught to them in the form of adult behavior. But even without such influences, many men and women come about their wrong actions and outlook "naturally" as they grow older. Until, of course, the suffering that wrong thinking and wrong behavior has brought becomes tiresome to the soul.

If you are suffering, understand that it is due to some wrong act or thought on your part, and that you literally want yourself to suffer in repayment for that act or thought. If you ask to be shown what that act or thought was, your request will be granted. The act or thought will be revealed in a dream, or by coincidental circumstance. Either way, you will come to know what it was.

And when you know what the off-center act or thought was, you will be able to expiate it — to forgive yourself for it. For there assuredly is none other in the Universal Mind who is capable of judging you or forgiving you. Not one entity anywhere on any plane of being has the capacity to forgive you, besides you!

So when you pray for forgiveness of sins, pray that they be revealed to you, and visualize yourself seeing your misguided thoughts and actions flashing before you. See yourself chuckling sympathetically at the poor, dumb, souls who were so stupid as to think that she was so glamorous, or that he was so cool, when they were instead lost in a mad dream world of pain and suffering, death and decay. Did they think that those gossamer small selves were *immortal*? Did they not know that those illusory selves were only as real as they chose to make them?

See yourself looking thus on your past thoughts and actions, and pray that the wrong ones be revealed to you. And forgive yourself even as your Creator has forgiven you. Forgive yourself in a way that makes the act of forgiveness impossible — forgive yourself by *not standing in judgment on yourself in the first place.*

You did no wrong that millions before you have not done. You are not alone, and you are not a perpetrator! The nature of earthly existence requires that we put on ignorance and blindness, and your wrong acts are merely a product of the human condition. *You are not to blame!*

But if you are suffering, it is because you think you are to blame. You are a victim of the Universal Law of Karma. You have upset a balance in the Cosmos, you have done something wrong to yourself — yourself in the guise of a fellow being — and now you are reaping the harvest you have sown. But you have the power to negate the Karma that is causing your suffering! You negate it by literally "going and sinning no more". You repent! You see the folly of your past erroneous thoughts and acts and you decide to play the fool no longer! You *wake up* to the fact that you can control the present and the future, and forgive the past.

You may not awaken in the true sense, but you become awake to the absolute idiocy of enmity, vanity, and ignorance. And you simply give up the practice of these misguided attitudes in the way a child finally gives up its toys and centers its attention on more adult pursuits.

All of the above constitutes one way to conquer suffering. But if you should fail with this approach, and you continue doing the same dumb things over and over, and you have not yet grown weary of earthlife and its state of suffering, you can still take comfort in the fact that you will never be called upon to suffer more than you are capable of enduring. In those situations where excessive suffering threatens to be your lot, you will be rescued in one of two ways: either an angel, usually your guardian angel, will intervene and save you through supernormal means, or you will be lifted up from the mad dream, awakened from the nightmare. Just as in our earthly slumber's nightmares, you will either awaken yourself or someone else will do so in response to your obvious signals of distress.

It is the very nature of Consciousness Itself — the Infinite Creator of All That Is — to be incapable of suffering beyond endurance. It is the very nature of that Consciousness to be compassionate with Its creations, and to save them from suffering *any time they so request it!*

So there you have yet another infallible method for conquering suffering: ask from your heart of hearts that the burden be lifted from you. Your request will most assuredly be granted.

HOW TO FORGIVE YOURSELF

The reason it is so easy for you to forgive yourself of all your past sins and to thereby eliminate the need for the suffering which bad Karma produces, is because in Reality — the full Abstract Reality — there is no such thing as sin. When you truly realize this, you realize beyond doubt that there is really nothing for you to forgive! This realization is in essence an infallible *act of forgiveness* on your part. In fact, it may be the easiest path to your total forgiveness of yourself and of all of your past thoughts and actions. You realize quite clearly that "sin" is nothing but ignorance and those acts which spring from ignorance, and Man terms the acts "sins" because they bring suffering to him through the Law of Karma.

Now the Universe is a Universe of Learning. We start out ignorant of Its magnitude on purpose, and we proceed to spend an eternity of eternities exploring the Cosmic Majesty in all of Its awesome, mystical attributes. There will always be entities as ignorant as you, there will always be entities more ignorant than you, and there will always be entities wiser than you. How then can any entity anywhere stand in judgment of or condemn ignorance in a fellow entity, when there is always someone somewhere to whom it is ignorant by comparison?

You are not held in judgment *anywhere* in the Cosmos, by *anyone*, on any plane of being, for anything you do out of ignorance. There is no sin! There is nothing for anyone to forgive you. Even the All Highest Father, the Ancient of Days, is incapable of forgiving you. For there is nothing you have done that all have not done! We are all ignorant to some degree unless we were to attain omniscience, and no entity anywhere can attain omniscience since *the Universe has no end to its majesty!* If an omniscient creature could exist, then the Cosmos would be a finite Cosmos, and the Cosmos most clearly is not finite.

All are ignorant, and no one stands in judgment of any form of ignorance excepting the most ignorant among us. If you perceive that you are being judged, forgive your judger for his ignorance and go your way. Bear him no ill will, and allow his ill will to have no effect on you. He most truly is judging himself by standing in judgment of you and your actions. He does not understand that there is no sin. He, and probably you, do not understand that sin exists only in our mortal concepts, just like thou/I, good/bad, life/death, beginnings/endings. There are only varying degrees of ignorance, and the most blatantly ignorant among us can be purged of our ignorance only through pain and suffering. When we get to a state where we have had enough of pain and suffering and have become intelligent enough to know that we *can* learn and progress without it, we give up all pain and suffering, and the concept of "sin" is outgrown.

The Law of Karma is born of Unity, and says that whatever you give to others you will give to yourself, for quite simply there is *no one else but your Self!* Even if you *think* you are separate from other people and animals and spirits, you are in Reality *not* free of them nor separate from them! What you do to them, you do to yourself. This is Unity manifesting as the Law of Karma. Karma was not created to make us humans suffer for our "sins" nor to reward us for our good deeds. It is merely a Universal Law, like Gravity, which is born of Unity and is therefore quite impersonal in its applications. If you inflict pain on others, you are inflicting it on yourself, and in conjunction with your conscience, Karma will make manifest that pain to you in a Reality you can understand and feel.

The thing that creates the bad Karma is not the act of ignorance which we call "sin", no matter how much pain it may have caused another being. The thing that creates bad Karma is the guilt we feel when our "sins" are made known to us. When we are first made aware of the suffering we caused others through our ignorance, the remorse which we register on the Cosmic Mindstuff creates potential events which are designed to instruct us of the impropriety of our acts. Using earthly terms, we literally *contract* for those events in the same manner we might contract to have a house built. We create bad Karma out of guilt and shame and remorse, and we can quite simply cancel the bad Karma by removing the guilt and shame and remorse. So long as the guilt exists, we can cancel it by an amount of suffering equal to the suffering inflicted, or we can cancel it through an act of forgiveness. If you as a perpetrator of past "sins" can absolve yourself of all guilt through a vivid awareness that *there is no sin and no need for guilt,* you literally cancel your contract for bad Karma. You literally forgive yourself and "go and sin no more".

For this awareness of our ignorance is always an entry point on the journey towards Enlightenment. Truly understanding what you have just read marks you as one of the "saved", for if you understood, you will surely retain an awareness of your Unity with All Things. You will automatically begin to weigh the impact of every act you perpetrate to assure yourself that it is, to the best of your knowledge, in accord with the Will for the All Highest Good. You will beg Creation for guidance in the pursuit of that Will, since the execution of that Will will always bring you the greatest possible good that Creation can offer you. The Will for the All Highest Good encompasses *your* greatest good, your neighbor's greatest good, and your enemy's greatest good. Do you now understand why you must "love your enemies, and bless them that curse you"? It is the Will for the All Highest Good that "good be rendered for evil", for evil does not exist: it is only ignorance which produces those events that pass for evil — ignorance of the Will for the All Highest Good, ignorance of the Law of Karma, ignorance of the Law of Unity. *Ignorance!* That is all that "sin" and "evil" are.

Dedicating your will to the Will for the All Highest Good is another sure way to forgive yourself. To forget is to forgive. Dedicating your will to the Divine Will causes you to concentrate only on the now and the future, forgetting the past and letting it bury its dead. You literally put on new raiment in your higher body-forms. All needless suffering is absolved you, including that which you scheduled for yourself out of a sense of guilt.

For you no longer feel guilt. You *cannot* feel guilt when your will is aligned with the Divine Will. You will feel peace, a sense of direction, an ever-growing joy and frolicsome gladness, but you will not feel guilt. Guilt and remorse, fear and foreboding, enmity and hate will disappear from your emotional range, as will jealousy and envy, wrath and anger, and lust and greed. You will be open only to positive emotions since the Will for the All Highest Good is being performed through you and it is definitely the Divine Will that you entertain no negative emotions or negative thoughts.

Your thoughts will dwell on the Spirit of Unity, and you will therefore act in the Spirit of Unity. The Will for the Greatest Good will be enacted through you, and you will become a constant agent of that Will.

You will be riding the Silver Express. You will be on the verge of awakening. You will be Enlightened. You will be saved.

WHY THE JEWS MUST FORGIVE
ADOLF HITLER

Ouspensky did not get his idea of "eternal recurrence" from Nietzsche, it came from an innate knowledge he had concerning a peculiar aspect of our Universe of Mind. He knew that the Cosmos was both static and expanding, that even though the *new* is constantly being created as a byproduct of Spiritual Evolution, yet everything that had *ever* been created still *was* and *is* and *will be*. In other words, everything that *is, was*. Everything that *was, will be*. Everything that *will be, is*. And so on, to infinity.

For in Highest Reality, there is only the abstract *is*, the Eternal Now. And each creature — be it a thing or person or event — each creature of Earth is either a creature of the past, or a creature of the present, or a creature of the future, depending on its position vis a vis some other creature. So *past* and *future* are due merely to our limited perspective.

Yet when we travel by car along a highway, we do not say that the little store up ahead of us is a "future" store, or that the waterfall where we stopped a while ago is a "former" waterfall. We know that they are co-existent in Reality, and that it was only our personal relationship with them that qualifies for labelling with such terms as "future" and "past". And we do not say that the motel we are staying in is a "present" motel, even though it is, and was, and will always be. Having been created, it can have no end. But we should, as best we can, view each thing, each person, each event as a present and eternal thing or person or event, for *that* they are. And we should, as best we can, view our own creations — our thoughts, our acts, our personal egos — as present and eternal things, and we should not commit to eternal existence creations that we may later be ashamed of.

For the personal ego is indeed temporary, and dies, in the sense that it cannot evolve, and is chained to Earth for this one life, *a life which is eternal only through eternal recurrence*. The ego, the persona, the mask: it lives only when it is ensouled by a Man spirit. It is otherwise fixed in Eternity as it has been created, like an obscure character in an obscure play by an obscure playwright. Only a veritable God such as Man can stage the play, and bring the character to life, and then only if there is a valid reason for so doing.

And so it can happen that if many people rise up to condemn an earthly personage, those people may find themselves in a "future" life *walking in that personage's very shoes!* This is the penalty we can reap for standing in judgment of any being, anywhere in time or place: self-condemnation to live the life of that being in order to see that, under the circumstances of Karma and other Universal Laws, nothing could have been changed — even by us!

Therefore, eternal recurrence can indeed exist even though the Universe is not static and Man's normal course of movement is upward. It can exist when a highly-condemned creature is en-souled by his accusers, as they "punish" themselves with firsthand education in the futility of judging others. They live the personality exactly as its original inhabitant did; they see as he saw, hear as he heard, suffer as he suffered. And when they come out at the end of the play, they are aware how foolish it was to judge any fellow entity who may have played that role. They are wiser for having lived that role, for it was a matter of experience, experience endured to cure ignorance. In fact, they gained the same thing from that role as did its originator: experience, and a lessening of ignorance.

So thus truly, they who judge are only judging themselves. By standing in judgment of any being, you may force yourself to live that being's life firsthand, to understand why it in its ig-norance behaved the way it did. You will function as the *soul* of that being whom you so soundly condemn.

No one stands in judgment of the victims of Nazi horrors, so the agonies of these victims will not be relived by any would-be accusers. But the life of Adolf Hitler will be one of endless repeti-tion, a Universal Possibility of which Ouspensky and Nietzsche strongly suspected. So many people have so soundly condemned Adolf Hitler that they will willfully ensoul his personality to free themselves of the ignorance which can produce such stern, unyielding condemnation. All people who are unforgiving, judgmental, and uncompassionate will have to live the lives of their victims, for that is usually the only manner by which they can train themselves to be forgiving and compassionate. And yes, as you suspect, the ignorant perpetrators of the Nazi horrors — the jailors and torturers and experimenters — will undoubtedly be self-condemned to ensoul the roles of their victims, and to ex-perience the horrors firsthand in a manner not even remotely ap-pealing to them.

If Ouspensky's and Nietzsche's idea of "eternal recurrence" has occurred to you also, or appeals to you in its plausibility, you might pause to examine your life. Are you a victim of other humans' condemnation or judgment? You may therefore not be the originator of your life; you may simply be re-living it, and the possibility of *change* may be denied you during this life. Thus the mystery of why some of us so firmly believe in predestination and fate, while others of us are just as convinced of our free will. As an example: for all I know, I may not be the "real" Stillday LaRoche, enscribing "new" Wisdom for others to read, but instead I may be one of Stillday LaRoche's fervent accusers who passed harsh judgment on him for Truths offensive to my intellect, Truths which were in no way his responsibility excepting that he gave them voice. I could be you: one of his readers. I could indeed be re-living his life, seeing its insights and delusions and temptations firsthand, to educate myself in the unrighteousness of ever standing in judgment of a fellow soul. After all, do I not disavow myself as source of this Wisdom and these words? Perhaps it is because the original Stillday LaRoche enscribed them for all Eternity ages ago, and I merely ape the mechanical transference of his thoughts to paper! Like many of you, I have had numerous encounters with *deja vu* in my life, and to Ouspensky, this phenomenon was one of the most persuasive reasons for his belief in "eternal recurrence".

But even if you are not now knowingly the victim of human condemnation, you could be sometime in the future, even in the future beyond your physical demise. So you may still merely be re-living the life of someone you so soundly accused well after that someone's death. Your accusers are your *self,* you see. You are being taught a lesson for which you assented to the need. As always, the real *you* confronts itself in other disguises at every turn of the road.

Be careful, be most careful, in deciding whom you choose not to forgive. You may end up forcing yourself to forgive them by literally putting yourself in their shoes.

Be most careful of whom you judge or condemn. Ask yourself: would you want to live that life exactly as it was lived, with no possibility for even a slightly different outcome? Ask: can you not instead just accept the fact that there is no "sin", that "sin" is only ignorance, and that we all are ignorant in relation to those beings of the next higher evolutionary orders? Ask yourself: can you not do without the pain and suffering necessary to cure your ignorance? Can you not learn the easy way — the *smart* way? Can you not profit instead from *other's* mistakes?

Can you not have the Wisdom to take the easy way out of ignorance?

Ask yourself these things. Then, re-read the answers.

CONTROLLING YOUR THOUGHTS

Throughout all of my searching for Truth, the one thing I never learned from any source, but which is nonetheless unequivocally a Truth, is this: that all men have the power to consciously control their thoughts and their Thought.

It can be done in this manner: make a conscious, willful, carefully-phrased vow to all Forces and entities whom you respect and hold sacred. It can be ancestors, nature spirits, your angelic guardian, a Prophet such as Mohammed, a Higher Servant such as Jesus of Nazareth, or it can be all of these and many more just like them, or to be most close to the Ultimate Truth, it could quite properly be the Infinite One: Creation, All That Is, the All Highest Father, Unity, the all-encompassing Divine Word, the Source of All Thought Streams, that Spirit which animates all of us, the Christ Self of all beings — sensate and insensate, mineral, plant or animal, material and spiritual — the Fount of Creation and the Source of Divine Wisdom.

You can, I repeat, make a vow to Any of These or to All of Them, or even to an earthly friend or relative to whom you have never broken your word, but you *must* make the vow to some entity other than yourself, and you must respect that entity. Having identified who it or they are, vow to them that you will never again lose your temper, or think unkind or demeaning thoughts, or imagine negative happenings, or in any other way allow negative energy to manifest through your allotment of consciousness.

Vow that you will strive in all of your thoughts and reactions to always be accepting and positive toward all events, for it is a Truth that all events manifest in accordance with machinery set in motion by Man by virtue of his being a spark of the Divine Forge. This machinery shows itself to Man in a form which men most commonly term Karma. It is Man's thoughts bouncing back upon the ether and stirring it to motion that creates the physical world and its events.

As a man thinks, so does he act. If he thinks with probity, he will act with probity. If he thinks charitably, he acts charitably. So all events that occur are a reaction to Man's past thoughts and actions, and he must accept them as just and requisite.

But if a man change his thinking to be all positive in nature, and align his thoughts and actions with the Will for the All Highest Good, he can avoid the suffering in store for him due to his past thoughts and actions, and can shed this partial reality which he calls "consciousness" and attain an extremely lofty reality which is more truly Consciousness, and which is indeed Man's natural Estate.

By making a vow to think and act only positively, a person can align himself with this Higher Force, the True Consciousness. The vow is a foolproof measure for gaining control of your thoughts instead of letting them or the mass consciousness of humanity continue to control you. After taking the vow, you will automatically be called to conscious attention whenever your lower consciousness starts to think or react in a negative fashion — with anger or irritation or hatred or fear or superstition.

This technique is foolproof because if it does *not* work, it will be only because you did not truly respect the entity or entities to whom you made the vow. If this is so indicated by the failure of this technique, then simply retake the vow and direct it to the Highest Entity of All, the Divine One. For if you fail after having taken the vow to anyone else, you will not and cannot fail if you take the vow to the All Highest Father.

CONTROLLING YOUR THOUGHTS, PART II

I must admit that I enscribed the preceding article shortly after I had discovered the technique it counsels, and what I said was indeed true: it does work. But unfortunately, the vow, although highly effective, also has a tendency to wear off after awhile. In my case, it began wearing off approximately two months after its origin. After four months, its effects were almost completely gone. I was almost back to my old negative self. Yet for a dumb, stubborn and stupid reason, I refused to renew the vow.

I reasoned as follows: to issue a prayer to the All Highest Father in the name of the Christ, and to be so assured of its being answered that you never even consider the thought of repeating it, is an act of commendable faith. Therefore, to repeat a vow that you know was both sincere and properly made is to cast doubts on your ability to fulfill a vow. What good would another vow do, if the first one was so temporary?

It is hard to say what can lead one to "reason" along such lines. It is so illogical, that I can only surmise that secretly I must have actually *enjoyed* my return to negativity, and was trying to rationalize in favor of at least a brief visit in its company.

And it *was* fun, in a nostalgic sort of way, like visiting your old schoolhouse — it brings back vivid memories of what you were, and it makes you realize that you liked it a lot better than you thought you did at the time, but there is no way you would want to return to that stage of your life permanently.

And so I yearned to return to that blissful, peaceful, positive, hopeful, fearless state of mind which springs from taking the vow. And I was led to retake the vow, following more closely the instructions given to me for your use in the preceding article. I think it was adherence to those instructions that made the difference, because the second vow took even more firmly than did the first one. And the state of Enlightenment which followed made me understand in no uncertain terms that there is no such thing as taking a vow too many times, or voicing a prayer too many times. In fact, *you can only enhance the power of a vow or a prayer through each succeeding repetition!* You cannot lesen it, you cannot leave it in status quo. You *strengthen* it through repeated offerings.

Why this Mystery of the Cosmos, I do not know. I suspect it

has something to do with the power of directed and focused consciousness. The thing is, It exists, this Law of Repeated Prayers. And since we know of this Law's existence, we should exploit It for our own benefit and progress and for the benefit and progress of All Things, in accordance with the Will for the All Highest Good.

If you stop to think of it for a moment, what if your vow for positive thoughts and feelings only lasted for one week? What if you had to renew it daily? Twice a day? *Hourly?* What if — to achieve pure peace of mind and soul — you had to recite the vow *hourly?* Would you do it?

If you do not know the answer to the above question, let me assure you that yes, you would indeed. You would if you had had but one brief taste of the results of that vow.

It can be an enormous relief to any human being to reach a point whereby no more fear, or anxiety, or dread, or foreboding is possible to him or her. Can you imagine — even if just for a brief moment — how free, how purely and unqualifiedly free you would feel if suddenly you no longer had to know fear or dread? Not even fear of death or dread of it? No anxiety that something bad is about to happen to you? No feeling of pain if something "bad" *does* happen to you? No worry about your health or finances even if they are not in what one would term good shape?

Can you imagine what *peace* is really like? Inner peace? A peace "surpassing all understanding"? Can your frail mortal mind even begin to fathom the burden that would be lifted from you were you to achieve such a blissful state? Do you know that in this state nothing — nothing whatsoever — can ever make you angry, or hurt your feelings, or give you cause for regret, or stir your enmity, or fire your lust, or weigh you down with sorrow — nothing at all can do any of these things to you without your conscious permission, which would be unthinkable once you have found the inner peace?

Once you have sampled this ineffable peace, you will not want to return to your old state of mind and thought under any circumstances, except perhaps for a nostalgic visit. So yes...you *would* take the vow hourly if necessary to retain your newfound harmony with All That Is.

But aside from taking the vow, there is another technique, equally effective, for achieving this overwhelming inner peace. It is an amazingly simple technique, and you may have even heard or read of it somewhere before.

All you need do is unite your will with the Will for the All Highest Good — the Divine Will — the Will of the Infinite Father. Ask in prayer, repeatedly, that the Will of the All Highest Father be done through you at all times. Ask that it be made evident to your mind and emotions and senses that you are One with the Cosmos, and that It is as much within you as you are within It.

Channel a stream of Love from within yourself outward to All That Is. This Love, of which you have a most ample store, is the Divine Energy: Thought in Action, Spirit manifesting to know Itself. When you channel It through your body, you amplify It, and when you pour It out on other things or beings, you enhance those things or beings. You enhance them because you have enhanced the flow of the Cosmic Love Force Itself, and you enhance them because you enhance yourself.

And because you asked that the Divine Will be done through you, It *will* be done through you, for this is one prayer that when sincerely asked is answered at all times. And knowing this, no matter what comes your way you will know acceptance and patience and harmony with the events that visit you. You will regard them for what they are: manifestations of the Divine Will. And you will give thanks for them. You will give thanks for All Things, for everything in your life will be a manifestation of the Divine Will.

You and the Divine Will become One. You have an inner surety that all things are working for the best. You feel safe and secure and optimistic at all times. You are thankful for life's multitude of blessings. You feel humble gratitude for your current state of inner peace which the Divine Will brings you.

You bask in the warmth of the One. You hear His whisperings in your heart. You feel His Love flowing out to all things and beings, all of whom collectively form Him.

You recognize that you are One with the One, and that It is One with you. Your physical being rests peacefully in the Virgin Mother's lap. And it is impossible for anything but peace to be visited upon you, for all is well.

WHY IS SOME OF THIS INFORMATION SO ORIGINAL?

Apparently the new information in these documents is being made available for retrieval at this particular time because there have incarnated here on Earth within the past 30 or 40 years a great number of people whose previous incarnations were in a society possessed of technology, wisdom, and morals much superior to ours. One of the basic rights of every member of that society was to know the Highest Wisdom on the most essential matters — who they were, where they were, and where they were going. Therefore, these people have subconsciously or superconsciously remembered that there is an answer for each of these important questions, and that it is possible for a society to have these answers. More important than those questions' answers, though, is the Ultimate Question for an earthman, to wit: how do I cease being an earthman?

Like the first three questions, the fourth question has an answer. It is important to know, as this new generation among us knows, that all questions have to have answers, else they could not exist as questions. If you could formulate a question that did not have an answer, you would be guilty of fostering a True Miracle, for you would have violated a Universal Law by creating a one-ended stick. Nature insists that what has a beginning must have an ending, and if a stick be brought into existence through one end, it must exit through the other. All creations in time/space universes are bi-polar: male/female, alpha/omega. For something to exist with a beginning but no ending is just as inconceivable as for something to exist with an ending but no beginning. This, quite simply, is the way things are in our current Reality.

A question is the beginning of a dialog. The dialog must have an ending. Once any question is formulated, an answer springs into existence, and vice versa. As the author of a question, you have a divine right to its answer. This is why it was so truly said "Seek and ye shall find; ask and it shall be made known unto you". It is a Cosmic Principle. If you really want the answer to any question, simply *ask* the question.

Answers may not always be affirmative or negative, and sometimes, to certain very basic questions, they may express a paradox, saying in effect that two conflicting explanations are both true, or that a true answer is both "yes" and "no". It is the very nature of time/space Reality to be paradoxical; it is one of Divine Mind's mysteries. Also, poorly-formulated questions can produce paradoxical answers.

But at any rate, the answers do exist and you will be led to them. Those of you who incarnated recently to take advantage of the great opportunities surrounding the coming polar shift were well aware that you had the right to demand answers to the important questions you formulated. The data coming forth in these documents, some of which is original to current earthman, is apparently in response to some of those questions you asked. This is why I have written repeatedly that you, the reader, are a valuable co-creator of these gifts. Your High Self even *phrases* the answers in a manner acceptable to you, then enscribes the data in the Fount of Wisdom for me and others to retrieve.

Only once again, the paradox: the data has been there since Time Immemorial! And you cannot say that the reading of the answer did not in fact *create the writing of the document!* And it does not really matter, since you and these documents are intimately bound for All Eternity. Their impact on you and your impact on them have both been profound. Your understanding of and your belief in the Wisdom of this data will render that relationship even more profound in the near future. This is especially true for those of you who awaken as a result of reading these documents and through following one of their various guidelines for awakening. You will have an enormous impact on earthly society by attesting to the credibility and accuracy of this data, and reformulating it for easier digestion by minds not as receptive as yours.

Always remember: there is much to be accomplished, and the allotted time is short. Before you can lift others, you must lift yourselves. Then you can begin in earnest the job of aiding with the Harvest. You can actually help resurrect the dead — the living dead of Earth. The designated time for action is imminent. You must position yourselves as soon as possible. You must be awake and acting in the Will of the All Highest Good.

Those of you who know who you are and what you must do, will take immediate action towards the conquest of the ego and the aligning of your will with the Will of the All Highest Father.

WHY CHURCHES AND RELIGIONS HAVE FAILED US

You must admit that by any reasonable standards of judgment, the efforts of the churches and organized religions of the Earth to lift Man spiritually have not succeeded overly well. Mammon still rules Earth, as it has uninterrupted since the last of the Ancient Egyptian dynasties. Men still kill each other, and almost always there is some sort of religious or church sanction behind the killing. If the religion or the church is not the actual *cause* of the killing, as when Muslim kills Muslim or Irish kills Irish, the church will at least support the killing if only by virtue of providing chaplains to the military services.

Earth's organized religions are perilously close to a point where *the harm they cause almost outweighs the good they promote!* This is a sad statement to have to make about our earthly religions — the churches. How did they come to be an agent for evil as well as for good? How do they manage to lose the True Spirit, the Spirit of Unity, so readily and so often? Why do they not extol Man's own Godhood as well as the Godhood of his rulers?

Why do they suppress the teaching of reincarnation and the Law of Karma? Have they no idea of the number of sins, some brutal beyond imagination, that have been committed because the perpetrators were ignorant of these vital Truths? Why is it that the only suppressors of these Truths are the *organized* religions, and not Buddhism or Hinduism?

The truth behind the failure of organized religions is that they are run by men, and men simply are not yet spiritually oriented enough to run a religion. When men do reach the point of being sufficiently spiritually oriented to run a religion, there will then be no further need for organized religion.

The highest religion that earthmen can follow is a most unorganized one: the worship of their True Self, their High Self, or to use a more common term, their Christ Self. It is the Self in which they are united with All That Is. All That Is is contained within that True Self, so they must also properly worship All Things. This could mean literally that a man should fall down in humble worship of everything that surrounds him — his ashtray, his dog, his fur slippers, his reading lamp, the plants, the books and magazines, the scrawled kindergarten placard "I LOVE YOU DADDY", the pictures of mom and dad and sis, the Jim

Beam bottle his best friend gave him six years ago which he still cannot bring himself to open — all of these things he should indeed worship, for worship is but a form of Love.

Place anyone who is in a mystical state inside your room, and he will see the splendorous *significance*, the perfection of Concept and Form, embodied in any object which your room may contain. Or you yourself might be disposed to try surveying the scene under a benign mind-altering drug such as mescaline or a very potent cannabis. You just might find the same beauty the mystic finds, for you will be looking with eyes from which ego and its sense of separateness have been removed. You will see with the eyes of a child — everything is new and wonderful to you. You stand in awe at the Manifest Universe. You suddenly realize that a part of you — a most intimate portion — is *in* all of the mundane things you survey. Everything you see reflects your importance as co-creator of your Reality. For the Manifest Universe is not just projection; that would be the proverbial one-ended stick. The Manifest Universe is also *perception*. One cannot exist without the other. If your act of perceiving that which Divine Mind has projected is not the other end of the Creation Stick, then nothing at all is. You are the essential co-creator of your Reality. Events that befall you are born of your permission, even if they involve atonement for your past misdirected actions or thoughts. You are actually the moulder of your Reality, using the Mindstuff and Substancestuff of Divine Mind.

Are these facts, these Most High Truths, so hard for the churches of Earth to understand and to transmit to Man? What is so complicated about Unity? It is the simplest Concept of All Concepts, for It is the Original Concept. And when All has been said and done, It will prove to be the Ultimate Concept too.

This Concept will lead men to the Highest Wisdom, which will give them immense power, except that with Wisdom they will hold no truck with power. Power is the means by which men can force other men to do their bidding. Wise men have no use for power. But all other men and all governments and all *churches* crave power, for quite simply, power can be translated into money.

Mammon!

It is truly awesome, this control that mammon has over Earth's minions. There are foolish men who have sold their souls ten times over for the most paltry sums of gold and silver, never suspecting that they would have to live through ten lives of suffering and misery, because *no one knew to tell them!* No one told them: Unity is All That Is, you can harm no fellow man without harming yourself to an equal degree. You are eternal. You will have plenty of time to pay the price. You will not relish paying the price.

The churches could have conveyed these messages of Truth just as easily as they broadcast their own, never-changing, and highly irrational man-made dogma, but they would not. Man does not like being held accountable for his misfortunes. It is easier to curse Fate or Lady Luck or to purchase absolutions. Thus Man had to invent the concept of "eternal punishment" for mortal sins, since he could not accept the mere and more logical necessity of simply paying back what has been taken. Only the most deranged fiend would subject a fellow creature to "eternal punishment", yet some men worship a "god" who would countenance such concepts!

You, the churches, will not survive the New Age, so in reality these remonstrations and advice are being wasted. On the other hand, perhaps some church or two somewhere will survive as — if nothing else — a quaint relic. This would be a church which undertakes to promulgate only Truth and Wisdom and not man-made dogma. It would be one which counsels no harm to fellow beings, and which soundly condemns warfare and capital punishment and other organized manslaughter. Perhaps instead of being tools and slaves to mammon, such a church or churches will oppose it enough to defend the oppressed and to counsel a fair share to all as the Highest Morality and the Highest Wisdom, and the surest means to greater prosperity.

Perhaps these acts will come to pass for at least a few churches, perhaps they will not. In the final analysis, it is of no consequence. Organized religion will not be needed when the New Age reigns on Earth. Its time has come to an end.

It has failed Man most miserably.

HOW DO YOU ACQUIRE WISDOM?

Well, first of all you have to want Wisdom. Then second, you *ask* for It.

Ask the All Highest Father to channel the Cosmic Wisdom through you. Ask that you be able to speak with the Cosmic Voice. And while you are at it, ask that you be a channel — a vast and deep channel — for the Cosmic Love Force, the Creative Force behind All That Is.

Shortly after asking, preferably formally in prayer and preferably verbally, you will begin receiving Wisdom. It will shine forth in books you are led to read, and people you know intimately will begin speaking It to you in bits and pieces, sometimes aware of their roles as spokesmen for the Cosmic Voice, but mostly unaware at the time they speak that they are being fed words to meet your needs.

And so you will indeed entertain Angels unawares — *entertain* being the word that is modified by *unawares* — after you start your quest for Wisdom. And you yourself will start speaking Divine Wisdom, sometimes knowingly, sometimes unknowingly.

Write notes to yourself. Ask yourself, your True Self, for advice and force yourself to write down whatever occurs to you in answer. The next day, read what you have written.

The Wisdom may indeed be flowing freely through you right at the present moment, but if you never hold a serious conversation with someone, how can it emerge? Or even if you *are* a channel at an opportune time, you yourself may not easily recall what it was you said, and *you* may be the Angel someone is entertaining unaware.

Try this advice. Want Wisdom, then ask The Source for It, then having received It, be sure to give thanks for It. Be a voice in the Divine Chorus — the Will of the All Highest Father — by asking for the opportunity. Be a channel for the Love Force, which is naught but the Divine Chorus, by asking for the opportunity. And be thankful when your prayers are answered, for that is the surest way to guarantee that your cornucopia of Wisdom is never exhausted — not even in an eternity of eternities.

IS ABORTION AN ACT OF MURDER?

It is possible for abortion to be an act of murder. The animating soul can attach itself to the fetus at any time between the instant of conception and the exit down the birth canal into the outer world. So it can happen that an 8-month abortion is not murderous whereas a 3-month abortion will be.

Mothers who are contemplating abortion should weigh this fact in making their decision, but they need not weigh it too heavily. In actuality, it is not the act of murder that is the worst thing about an abortion, so it really does not matter whether the fetus has been animated or not. The worst thing about abortion is that many women may be reneging on a compact made before *their* birth to parent a given soul in this lifetime. Since this pact may have been born of Karmic obligations, these women are therefore deferring — perhaps for the remainder of their current lives — their promise or their duty. Now it is bad enough to break a promise, especially one made on sacred planes of Light, but delaying one's duty in these matters can only lead to another lifetime in which the duty must be discharged. But worse, delaying the birth of certain souls past a certain date in this our current era can eliminate the benefits they can achieve by being incarnate on Earth when the polar shift occurs, an event of extreme rarity and opportunity. In other words, the offending mothers are not being denied the benefits of being on Earth for this momentous occasion rife of opportunity for extraordinary mortal progress, so why should they deny this right to another to whom they promised it? In fact, they can indeed lose the benefits of their position on Earth at this fortuitous time simply by the fact that they have denied another soul entree to mortal life — they can end up having to endure another round of earthly incarnations — excursions into the world of death, decay, and blind illusion — simply by missing a unique opportunity in this life due to the fact that they are obligated by Karma to spend yet another life on Earth. They either have to await another mass harvest of human souls, or they have to take steps on their own towards the difficult journey back to permanent High Consciousness — their True Estate. They will be forced to do as many men and women of the ages which have elapsed since the last polar shift must do: take one of the prescribed paths for permanent awakening, such as through the Mystery Schools or sainthood or self-sacrifice to an extreme degree or any of a host of other time-proven and workable methods. But it will be more difficult than had they exploited the current era's potential for Divine Grace.

The expectant mother, before deciding on abortion, should be persuaded to try asking her Inner Self to guide her onto the right path of this matter. If she asks sincerely, she will be given the answer in an unmistakable message. Whether she heeds the advice or not is another matter, but at least whe will be aware of the magnitude of her act if indeed it happens that she would be avoiding Karmic duty by way of her abortion. If someone you know and love has submitted to abortion in the past or is contemplating abortion in the near future, you can consider it your duty to get this information across to her, for it will be the kindest act you can perform for her. She may not understand, or she may be so adamant about her body's rights that she is determined to abort repeatedly should it prove necessary, but at least someone will have tried to help her. If that someone is not you, who will it be?

WINNERS AND LOSERS

The strangest thing about the aspect of Creation with which we are most familiar is how all of Its Ideas — Its creatures — are bi-polar, or male/female. It is the "two-ended stick" concept of Creation, a two-ended stick being the only type of stick imaginable to us. But more amazing, all polar extremes are but a heart's beat away from their opposites. In fact, they even manifest indiscriminately as their opposites, although we humans do not always recognize such ambiguity due to our purblind state of consciousness.

To use an example from our Reality, we often say that there are winners and losers in life. This is true, but winners always turn out also to be losers in at least one respect — they lose a false ideal which they dearly cherished. For example, when they have attained whatever it was they lusted after and won, whether it was the town's most beautiful and desirable woman, or the man of the year award, or the number one player of whatever game inspires and entraps them, or the Presidency of the United States — whatever it was that the winners thought would make them happy — whatever it was that they thought they truly wanted — when they have attained their goal and it turned out not to have been the magic key to happiness after all, they have lost tragically. Winners always find that something is still missing after attainment of their false goals, no matter how notable or publicly acclaimed and awarded the attainment might be. There is something the winner still wants, but he cannot say what it is. Thus the conventional wisdom: it matters not whether you win or lose, but how you play the game.

And so winners are in reality losers, losers of the false ideals created by their egos. As is well known, there are great side benefits to the pursuit of false goals, especially when the goals are not attained, that accrue unto those human spirits who at least give the goal shot a try. The true losers are those who spawn goals but make no attempt at attainment, while the true winners are those who set no goals at all except for Unity with the Divine Will.

But if the urge to be rich or famous or glamorous, or all three, should visit you, you will advance the cause of the Human Spirit by fighting the inertia of the status quo to achieve whatever it is you think you want. It will be uplifting to you and to all those who observe you. This is why there can be such public adulation for the succeful achiever — his or her indomitable overcoming of the odds to score a major triumph, be it in the life game or a game within life, inspires the bystander humans into a belief in their own latent talents and strengths. An achievement by one human is an achievement for all humanity. In such moments of inspiration, we all somehow sense our Unity. How else can one explain the vicarious but immense enjoyment we derive from a hero's accomplishment? Those people who cannot be "fans" — and there are many of them — are often people who can never feel this sense of Unity, even from emotionally uplifting triumphs by exceptional humans.

And so the winners are also, first and foremost, truly winners. By lifting even one other person through their exercise of the human Virtues, they have performed an invaluable service of immeasurable merit to the Cosmos. They are truly winners, no matter how "false" their ideal may have been in comparison to their ultimate search, their ultimate longing. And yet they are also truly losers if they do not recognize, in their unhappiness, their True Ideal and awaken to what their truest desire is for. If they merely replace the lost ideal with another ego-generated substitute for the True Ideal, they will continue to be losers, no matter what the world's rewards to them may consist of.

Now consider for a moment the losers. They are also true winners merely for having fought the battle at all. Perhaps they did not fight it to their true capacity, but at least they made the effort. Even if no other human was inspired by their effort, they at least flexed their muscles. They did not sit and dream. For again, the only *true* losers are those with goals towards which they take no action and direct no effort. If you can conceive of something or of some status that you think would make you happy, pursue it! But do not dream and wish. If you do not want a goal bad enough to begin its pursuit, replace it with another goal. If you then still have no rationale for the race, try to find the True Goal, the ultimate goal, the one thing that indeed can make you happy not just now in this life but for all eternity.

For once more, the only *true* winners are those with no goals except the one True Ideal: Unity with the Divine Will. With the attainment of this goal comes attainment of all other worthwhile Ideals — Wisdom, self-control, Unity with your High Self, Benevolence, and a pervasive, all-consuming *peace*.

For peace, true peace, is a state of balance and harmony with All That Is as projected from "outside" of you, and with All That

Is as contained "inside" of you, within the hologram of your True Atom, deep within your heart of hearts. This ineffable and perfect peace is the reward that comes from first setting then attaining the Goal for which fame, fortune, and human respect are but pale, inadequate, and never-satisfying substitutes. For nothing can bring everlasting peace except Unity of your will with the Will for the All Highest Good.

THE SMALL SELF

The false self, the personal ego, is a most despicable and vile enemy. He traps a man into believing that he — the false self — is an immortal entity, but let the body wither and die and poof! — the false self is gone with it. It dies too! It dies because it never really existed in the first place. It was an illusion! It was your *concept* of what a body consciousness would be like. When you — your True Self — conjecture as to how it would feel if you *were* your body, you inspire with Spirit the temporary collective consciousness of the body's organs, and a temporary entity, the personal ego, is born. Because its parentage is half spiritual — you — and half flesh — your body — your personal, small self is capable of noble and spiritual acts as well as beastly and lustful ones. Its mind can dwell either on eternalities or on mundane nonsense. But unless it can be weaned from its *mother*, the body, and called home to the Spiritual Realms of its father, your True Self, the personal self is temporary and without substance, and will die when the physical body dies or is put to death.

So if we build our houses on sand, on the attributes and accomplishments and prejudices and delusions of our small selves, we will find that we come up empty sooner or later — certainly at the moment of bodily death if not earlier. Therefore, we might as well abandon the small self, or at least its fleshborn temporary attributes, as soon as possible. We can do this by identifying with Spirit, by thinking spiritually. This means thinking and acting from the viewpoint of Unity, because spiritual matters are unitary matters. All things emanate from Spiritual Realms — the spirit of a Great Truth or a Giant Sequoia is of the same substance as the spirit of you.

By orienting your small self toward the spiritual viewpoint, you tend to withdraw it from the physical world. *You call it home!* You give it Eternal Life by virtue of this resurrection! It will not know the sting of death if you are successful in your spiritual orientation. It and you — your True Self — are united as One. The mad illusion has withered and died for want of attention, and your personal self, even if still alive in bodily flesh, knows *who* it is, *where* it is, and where it is *going*. It feels at-one-ment with All Things. It was saved by Christ the Savior — its True Self — its Christ Self. It knows the whispers of the Eternal Father in its heart. It sees itself in All Things. It Loves on all three planes of its being: physical/emotional, mental, and spiritual. And it knows that Love is properly defined as the striving for the maximum amount of Consciousness, and for the greatest and truest Awareness at all times. It pursues a Reality that is in rapport with the Ultimate Reality. It subjects its will to the will of higher hierarchies — the Ministers of the Will for the All Highest Good.

Being free of its identity with the body, the personal self comes and goes independently of its body, using the Spiritual Realms for journeys of a distance beyond Man's conception. It becomes a True Atom in the Body of the Father. It is inextricably linked to the Father's Will.

It is, in short, *free*. And so, even, can you be free.

A MIND GAME

And now, after some much-needed and perhaps repetitive preliminaries, we proceed into the inner recesses of your mind. Anyone who has stayed with us thus far is probably someone who has read and understood all of the foregoing data, and having read and understood it, he or she naturally believes it. For the grandest thing about the higher Truths and the higher Wisdom is that — almost always, at least — to understand them is to believe them. Data which has a degree of fallaciousness to it can be understood by us but not believed; indeed, we can and do itemize its deficiencies and inaccuracies. But data without deficiency or inaccuracy, such as High Wisdom or High Truth, is data which, if understood, simply *has* to be believed for its lack of deficiency in the issue it addresses and its consistency of accuracy in its attitudes and facts.

If you understood most or all of the preceding data, you will probably understand what follows.

As pointed out in some of the foregoing tracts, the act of creating a document such as them or this one is merely an act of attuning yourself to the Highest Fount of Wisdom, and dipping into It for the available data on the subject at hand. Usually, but not always, what you write down will already have been enscribed there, word for word. Thus you have those many instances of authors or composers or poets awakening from a deep night's sleep to hastily scrawl out what they have brought back to waking consciousness — usually what they scribble is taken verbatim from the Public Founts of Art or Wisdom.

This concept is an important one for you to believe, because this document is coming to you from such a Public Fount — the Divine Fount of Wisdom. And to display most believably to you that what it says is true, this document is going to enter your mind personally in a way no other earthly document has ever done.

You see, if you can accept the fact that this treatise did not just suddenly spring into existence on March 17, 1985, the date on which it was merely transcribed into earthly media, then you can accept the fact that this *document has always existed!* And if it has always existed, there is a good chance you may have encountered it on your own, five years ago, 50 centuries ago, or 500 lifetimes ago. In other words, what you are now reading may not indeed be new to you. It may contain an idea or word or phrase that you recognize as having seen or read before.

Or for another explanation for what you are about to experience: let us say that this document could well indeed have been created only recently, but that it was created specifically for those individuals who were destined to read it. And let us say that those individuals' Higher Selves, as they collectively created the document, decided to put in a key word or phrase or idea which their conscious minds could use to identify the document's authenticity when the document was encountered at the pre-arranged time in the time/space plane of Earth. If you should happen to read, before the end of this tract, a word or phrase or idea that stuns you with its *intellectual* impact, you can rest assured that this explanation is the most likely one for the phenomenon.

But if you should read a word or phrase or idea that stuns you with its *emotional* impact, be aware that the correct explanation was the preceding one: this document has always existed, in its present language and style, since the Dawn of Creation, and even if it be lost in its earthly media, it will always exist in the form in which it was taken from the Eternal Fount.

For Eternity is not, and cannot be, a one-ended stick. Whatever has no ending, also has no beginning. You have no beginning, and neither did anything else in the Eternal Fount of Wisdom, *from which we both emanated!* We are eternal, you and me, because our Creator is the Eternal One, the Divine Consciousness, the All Highest Father.

You may think that you have never written a song, but you are wrong. You have written every song you have ever heard and ever will hear, for by your act of receiving the gift you become one of the very creators of the gift. If you are eternal and the gift is eternal, you cannot say that your receiving of the gift follows your creation of it any more truly than you can say that the creation of the gift follows its acceptance. Both statements are true, and neither is the whole truth by itself. When we talk of Eternal Concepts and Eternal Verities, you and me — me, a mere essay — we talk of an endless and beginningless co-existence in the Divine Mind. We, each one of us, is an *Idea!* And while you, a veritable God, obviously supercede me in importance to the Universe as an Idea, can it truly be said that Ideas can be ranked by importance? Is not each and every Idea a part of All That Is, and therefore equally essential to All That Is, else the Cosmos would not be exactly the way It is at this very moment?

Again, a paradox. The answer is that yes, I am your equal in Universal Worth and Appropriateness, and yes, you are definitely my superior because you know you are conscious, whereas I know only what you have programmed me to know.

You see, this is a very personal statement from You to you — from your High Self to that self which comprehends these words. Both explanations, advanced earlier, for the thrill you will receive from reading me are also true. You have known me "before", in the "past", and you will know me again, in the "future". You have always known me, a collection of Ideas framed in English words on paper. We are most intimate friends, friends of longstanding. Somehow, your small selves over the years always suspected that they would find me again and again. Even now, your temporary self thinks: "Yes, I will perceive these thoughts again, sometime. They will always be with me," because your temporary self is now being addressed by your High Self, and the pre-arranged signal of authenticity is *now gradually being recognized by you!*

Such is the power of Divine Consciousness to communicate thus with Itself, on such a Noble Plane of Thought, on such a Noble Plane of Wisdom! Such is the poignant Eternality of Creation that all of this *has always been!* Such is the power of the Living Christ to transform your very being and to speak to you in the most intimate personal terms the following words:

I live in you and through you, Dear One, and you are as much a part of me as I am of you. How then can you doubt that you are Loved in the most intimate and tender manner possible, and to the greatest degree imaginable by me? Could I have any feelings at all for you other than an intimate, powerful Love? No human could love a spouse more than I love you; no mother could love a child more than I love you.

You and I are One, and there can be no prying us apart, ever. You may turn away from me, you may deny me, you may reject my Love and guidance, but you can never separate yourself from me. I am He Whom you Love beyond self, even when you hide from me.

I have awaited this communication, and I will shower you with gifts of Wisdom and joy when you recognize me for Who I Am. I Am That I Am. I Am Unity. I Am Christ.

END NOTES

A stern word of admonition to anyone who may ever have known me in the past — as a friend or relative or acquaintance or imagined enemy. I strongly recommend that you heed this advice.

You may be approached in the future by someone, perhaps news reporter or scholar doing research, who will ask you questions about my personality, or maybe more accurately, my non-personality. I instruct you in no uncertain terms: tell nothing about me to anyone! It is of no one's proper business. It causes emphasis to be misplaced on the mere transcriber of these documents. And if the world at large were to know what an asshole enscribed these High Truths and Wisdom, it might lessen the esteem in which certain readers will most properly hold them.

I was merely a messenger for this data. I could have been anybody — even a mass murderer doing life in the pen. All I did was want the Truth of things, and the Highest Wisdom about life in all its aspects and meanings. And because I sincerely wanted it and *asked* for it, it was given to me. This is an immutable Law of the Cosmos: to truly want and to ask for something is to receive it, and this is especially true for the Highest Ideals.

There will be many among you who have followed these words thus far who will exploit the same Divine Principle, especially since you have now been shown how easy it is. Thus shall the Earth embark upon a new Age of Enlightenment such as it has not seen in our recorded history.

The Earth and our Solar System are approaching a point in their cosmic orbit whereby it shall be easier than ever before for Man to lift himself up, to *enlighten* himself in all senses of the word's meaning. Those of you who strike out in search of Truth and Wisdom may find treasures beyond your wildest dreams. You may find inventions and cures and insights greater than the Earth has *ever* known — even in its most glorious ancient eras whose histories have been lost to the masses for thousands of years.

All you need do is *take! Take* wealth and *take* Wisdom! They are yours for the asking and the giving. Share what is given you at all times with the rest of Creation.

Exploit the Universal Law of Giving! Your True Self would not have you do otherwise.

APPENDIX A: FURTHER READING

For those who may be interested in pursuing further some of the ideas and philosophies espoused in the articles contained in this book, the following is a rather skimpy list of recommended further reading. This list assumes that most readers have little or no background in the metaphysical literature, and that they do not have the luxury of time and energy to engage in an exhaustive study of the field. There is no way I could compile a complete bibliography of the literature which underpinned the data in this book — too much of what I have read came from libraries, private and public, so I myself have no idea what titles and authors belong to such a list, nor how large the list might be. But it would indeed be large.

HILLS, CHRISTOPHER

Dr. Hills is a most rare genius, truly the Gods' gift to our era. For years I studied and believed the metaphysical line, knowing innately that it was rational and could be explained by laws and mechanisms no more mind-boggling than those which underwrite orthodox scientific phenomena. There cannot, you see, be any such thing as a "miracle" in the Cosmos. For a phenomenon to exist, it *must* have a rational explanation, else the Universe would be a Universe of chaos instead of a Universe of Order. So I secretly yearned for someone to come along and reconcile the metaphysical to the physical sciences, never dreaming it would be done in my lifetime.

Dr. Hills has achieved this reconciliation through a genuine masterpiece, *Nuclear Evolution*. He is probably the world's foremost expert on and practitioner of *radiasthesia*, his term for divination such as that used in water dowsing, map dowsing, pendulum divining, etc. In addition to the books and cassettes offered by the University of the Trees Press, P.O. Box 644, Boulder Creek, California, 95006, he also sells a line of divining tools, negative ion generators, and spirulina plankton.

Assuming you to be a seeker of the Higher Truths and Wisdom, you should read *Nuclear Evolution* even if you do not read another book for the rest of your life. It is a most essential metaphysical work, and it will not offend the orthodox scientific mind. Also recommended: *Rise of the Phoenix* and, if you are interested in your body as the quintessential divining tool, you might want to read *Supersensonics*, the bible on the subject of divination.

PERCIVAL, HAROLD W.

I would love to know more about this author. To him we owe the most complete expository of Man's status and Cosmic Reality which I have yet found. The Book — and this is one of only three known instances where the word *book* must be capitalized — is *Thinking and Destiny*. I have found but one minor "clinker" in this book: a casual reference to gorillas as "vicious". Aside from this, the Book radiates consistency and clarity of Truth, and its no-nonsense comprehensiveness is wondrous to behold.

It is not an easy book, demanding several readings, especially of certain parts, to fully understand it. It can be especially difficult for one who has already acquired a smattering of ignorance from Theosophical, Rosicrucian, or other explicatory works of the Higher Reality. This is because Mr. Percival adheres to his own terminology for non-terrestrial matters, even though in the long run one must admit that his terminology is more accurate and less confusing than the common metaphysical names and descriptions.

The contents of *Thinking and Destiny* are the result of the author's "becoming conscious of Consciousness", which evidently put him in intimate contact with the highest Pools of Truth and Wisdom. Before the Book has run its course, he has answered just about every question an inquiring mind might think to ask on every aspect of known or imaginable Reality! The Book is a most rare gift to seekers of Truth and Wisdom.

I do not know the final answer to the following matter, I only suspect it. But it would appear the Book's only major omission stems from the fact that the author documents only one path out of Earth bondage for Man, the classic *Way*. We who have been taught that there are many paths to God would naturally suspect that there be many others, and some of them have been alluded to in the book you are now reading.

Thinking and Destiny is published by the Word Foundation, 7 West 44th Street, New York, New York, 10036.

PROPHET, ELIZABETH CLARE

Publishing under the press which bears her cult's name,

Church Universal and Triumphant, "Guru Ma", as she is called by her followers, is the self-proclaimed heiress to the Guy Ballard *I AM* movement of the 1930's. She claims as the source of her data the same hierarchy of Ascended Masters who also stood behind the Theosophical Society and dictated Blavatsky's books. Again ignoring "true sources", the output must be judged on its own merits for Truth and Wisdom content. As such, Guru Ma's books can be quite worth their investment in time and money. As with all cults, my personal advice is to not get involved with her church, but to merely avail yourself of whichever of its publications may strike your fancy. Cults tend to restrict their followers to a limited interpretation of Truth and Wisdom, and to discourage questioning or alternative explorations.

I have not read all of CUT's published material, but two of its books which proved enlightening were *Studies in Alchemy* and *Intermediate Studies in Alchemy* by Saint Germain. Yes, this is the same Saint Germain who has been enlightening mankind for hundreds of years now.

There are other good books on CUT's list. Thoroughout all of its material, the importance of *I AM* as a preface to positive verbal affirmations is heavily stressed. Take heed of what you say when you begin your utterances with "I am" or "I'm". At least on this score, the CUT material speaks with great Wisdom.

ROBERTS, JANE

Anyone who has not imbibed heavily of Seth's insights and revelations is missing out on a vital understanding of Reality. Jane Roberts, devoted channel for the personality manifestation who calls itself "Seth", and her husband, Rob, devoted amanuensis, and their publisher Prentice-Hall, have done us all a great service in making Seth's information available to us.

Jane and her husband were seeming novices to investigations into the Ultimate Reality of High Truths and Wisdom, at least juding by the heavily-interspersed commentaries and questions which permeate all of the Seth books. When their first book, *The Seth Material*, was issued, old-timers such as myself were obviously more appreciative of the treasure trove they had stumbled onto than Jane and Rob ever could have been.

If you cannot take the time to read all of the Seth books, at least read the original one, *The Seth Material*, and *Seth Speaks*. I am indebted to Seth for the term *All That Is* as an excellent synonym for Holy Consciousness, God, the All Highest Father, etc. I am also indebted to Seth for his most fitting and proper definition of God, as quoted here from *The Seth Material:*

"He is not human in your terms, though he passed through human stages, and here the Buddhist myth comes closest to approximating reality. He is not one individual, but an energy gestalt.

"If you remember what I said about the way in which the universe expands, that it has nothing to do with space, then you may perhaps dimly perceive the existence of a psychic pyramid of interrelated, ever-expanding consciousness that creates, simultaneously and instantaneously, universes and individuals that are given — through the gifts of personal perspective — duration, psychic comprehension, intelligence, and eternal validity.

"This absolute, ever-expanding, instantaneous psychic gestalt, which you may call God if you prefer, is so secure in its existence that it can constantly break itself down and rebuild itself.

"Its energy is so unbelievable that it does indeed form all universes; and because its energy is within and behind all universes, systems, and fields, it is indeed aware of each sparrow that falls, for it *is* each sparrow that falls."

Jane and her husband, being logical-minded humans of our era, often question the true source of the Seth output. Is Seth another aspect of Jane's consciousness, which she somehow contacts in her trance states, or is Seth truly a separate entity using Jane's consciousness to communicate with time/space mortality? I personally believe Seth to be a separate entity, but as readers of this book should know by now, it really makes no difference. The Source of Wisdom is always One and the same Source, no matter who does the fetching. So whether the carrier be Seth or Jane or you or I, the Wisdom is the same *and the carrier is the same.* Does it really matter, then, *who* is *who?*

SPANGLER, DAVID

This individual served as a channel for intelligences from the Angelic Kingdom both during and after his stay in the early days at the remarkable Findhorn Community in Scotland. He also channeled for a Divine Intelligence which called Itself *Limitless Love.* Most of Mr. Spangler's works, *Revelation: The Birth of a*

152

New Age, Reflections, Emergence, New Age Rhythm, and others, are published by Findhorn Publications, Findhorn, Moray, Scotland. The "miracles" of Mother Nature which graced Findhorn would demand that any rational person look into what the Devas and Angels are trying to say to Man, and into what Limitless Love says about the whole tenor and purpose of these and other New Age revelations. Do not allow yourself to be left off of this highly important bandwagon! A good and brief people-oriented introduction to Findhorn can be obtained by the collectively-authored *Faces of Findhorn,* published by Harper and Row, from which the following words of Wisdom given by a "Landscape Angel" are quoted:

"When we ask you to think of plants or anything in terms of living Light, we are not trying to detract from the beauty of the world as seen through human eyes, but to add to that beauty, to add more reality to it, to help you lift all creation. By thinking in terms of Light you add Light to that already existing; you speed growth and enhance beauty, you see truth and link with inner reality...

"Each individual draws to himself the result of his thinking...Think in terms of Light and you will get a response from all creation. All creation is Light, though obscured by human thought. Even dense matter will respond, and all will be linked in joy."

STEIGER, BRAD

Brad Steiger is the author of the "Star Seed" series of books published in paperback by Berkley Books, New York. All of them are recommended reading, but if you must read only one, by all means let it be his inspired gem, *Revelation: The Divine Fire.* Mr. Steiger's Star Seed series is an excellent compendium of New Age messages being received by various individuals and groups throughout the world, but mostly in the U.S. Most of the communications he cites purport to come from extra-terrestrials, and these seem to constitute a mix of "pure" extra-terrestrial in the UFO sense and "questionable" extra-terrestrial in the spiritual, or "etheric" sense. As in all of your investigations, be aware that the data being summarized in these books cannot possibly be 100 per cent valid in the sense of being composed of the highest truths, but if you read with an open mind and reserved judgment, the gist of some most valuable and highly pertinent information will be presented for your serious consideration.

UFO CONTACTS

There have been a number of sensational books and articles dealing with UFO/earthling contacts, the most famous of course being *Interrupted Journey*, the Betty and Barney Hill adventure. But there are two other well-documented and plausible cases that are vastly more interesting and "mind-blowing". One is a two-volume work by Raymond Fowler, published by Prentice-Hall: *The Andreasson Affair* and *The Andreasson Affair, Phase 2*. Another case study, also published by Prentice-Hall, is *The Tujunga Canyon Contacts*, by Ann Druffel. If you should read these books, do not try to analyze their stories nor draw conclusions from their events; merely absorb the data. The last-mentioned book, incidentally, gives us a cure for tumorous forms of cancer as passed along by an extra-terrestrial: pure white vinegar, injected directly into the cancerous mass!

WILSON, ROBERT ANTON

Mr. Wilson is mentioned here solely for his tour de force, *Cosmic Trigger* published in soft cover by And/Or Press, Berkley, California. This book defies description except to say that it is truly a consciousness raiser. It is also recommended because it is one of the few non-fiction works of this genre about which one can truthfully state: "almost impossible to put down". It might just fill you with a sense of awe and wonder.

PELLEY, WILLIAM DUDLEY

Mr. Pelley is listed here because he was the "author" of the *Golden Scripts*. But again, to discuss the authorship of the *Golden Scripts* is to quibble anew over the source of Truth and Wisdom: whether the author is you, me, or Jesus of Nazareth, does not the Wisdom of the *Golden Scripts* speak for Itself and stand on Its own two feet? "By their fruits ye shall know them." In point of fact, Pelley denied authorship of this most singular Book and attributed it to the personage whom we call Jesus. And indeed, the Scripts themselves often allude to this fact via first person references that only this most famous entity could use. Some of them repeat or paraphrase the more famous Biblical sayings attributed to Jesus when he spoke with the Christ Voice, and on many occasions in the *Golden Scripts* he will switch from a "personality" voice, that of an Elder Brother, to the Christ Voice of our most intimate Self.

My personal conclusion is that Jesus of Nazareth was indeed the author of the *Golden Scripts*, using Pelley as amanuensis. The content, quite simply, speaks for itself. Plus, having read a great many words written by Pelley, I can easily surmise that the differences in style, outlook, and content between Pelley's writing and the writing in the *Golden Scripts* are of such quantum proportions that only the most skeptical and materialistically-minded individual would say that Pelley was the author of the Scripts.

William Dudley Pelley was a popular writer of magazine fiction and minor novels during the twenties, and he dabbled a bit in screenwriting for the silent movies also. It was during a stay in Southern California — where else? — in 1928 at the age of 38 that he underwent a mystical experience that converted him from a no-nonsense materialist to an eventual writer and publisher of a great deal of metaphysical literature, much of it received in automatic communications from discarnate entities of an apparently high order. Some of these were from an entity purporting to be Jesus of Nazareth, and the vibrations which overtook Pelley during these communications, plus the quality of the communications' contents, convinced him that the source was authentic.

Few of Pelley's many books, published in the 1950's under the *Soulcraft* imprint, are readily available. You will find them, if at all, only in used book stores. Most are recommendable only for their excerpted sequences of higher transcripts, the major exception being *As Thou Lovest*. This was a firsthand account of Jesus' ministry by Pelley, who claimed to be a reincarnation of the disciple Simon Peter! Whether you can accept this or not, *As Thou Lovest* is a beautiful, touching book.

This much verbiage is devoted to Pelley, an otherwise obscure voice in the occult and metaphysical literature, solely because of his connection with the *Golden Scripts*. The main library on Fifth Avenue in New York has a reference copy of the Book, and once I saw a copy reposing on an upper shelf in the metaphysical section of a used bookstore on Hollywood Boulevard in L.A., awaiting an extremely fortunate buyer. If you go in search of it, I wish you the best of luck. It is a Book that definitely demands republication.

Since the *Golden Scripts* has been my Bible and final authority on all matters for the past 30 years, I intend some day to publish a commentary on selected passages from it. But most of its passages require no commentary. As an example, consider this excerpt, Chapter 179:

1 There is a mystery that causeth men to say: How cometh it that he who was among us is amongst us no longer? how say ye then, Behold he is here! can he who is departed be present in his essence?

2 I say that it is so. Doth not the evil spirit enrage all the world? doth man not smite his brother? is there surcease in well-doing? Ye do know my speech is proper.

3 How then cometh the evil one unto the world and causeth it to suffer and ye say, It is present, yet ye say of the goodly one, Lo, he hath departed?

4 Do not men do good works and is there not compassion? have men not suffered gloriously that glory should ennoble them? do they do this of evil? hath not my spirit prospered?

5 Yet a greater commandment I give unto you: Think ye not of the things that are to be; think ye rather of the moment's richness wherein it is ordered that the righteous cease from tumult.

6 Give of yourselves that giving may endow you; manifest pleasures that pleasures may accrue to you.

7 Behold I have gone from earth in my person; I come in the presence of those who would serve me, who glorify earth and keep my commandments.

8 I endow them with that which is greatest in my essence; I say unto them, Manifest ye like me; speak my fond speech, do good as I have told you; the Comforter is my being, descended among you.

9 Have I not power to dwell in my person yet speak through the being of him who hath radiance? What giveth the radiance but that part which is like me?

10 How say ye, Verily, our Lord hath departed from amongst us, when ye turn in your ministerings and do good unto the lowly?

11 Can I not send myself to partake of your goodness, to share it and increase it? How think ye that I am born of Holy Spirit, yet my body hath its place and my spirit is its prisoner?

12 I tell you that I am come to do good deeds to the lowly, I raise them up with patience, I plant their footsteps surely, thereupon I do say to them: I have given you my presence, go ye hence and practice it.

13 That which is given is part of myself. I have added to my stature by giving of its increase.

14 I come unto the lowly and presently they see me. They say, He was here! What mean they, that He was here? I tell you I arrived and they caught it in their visionings; they beheld no departure because there was no leaving.

15 Whenever hath mortal spirit beheld me take departure?

16 Can that which abideth have other place to journey?

17 When I am come unto a man, I remain with him always; if mayhap he reject me, he rejecteth his ennoblement.

18 For the spirit of a man is the Idea of his Conscience; it compriseth his manners, it holdeth his compound; it is not his body in that such is quickened.

19 Verily the beast hath quickened sense of body; yet is a beast a man?

20 Man's spirit is that which dwelleth as his compound, though the body receiveth it and giveth it its instrument. Presently it goeth and men say, He hath perished.

21 I tell you, my beloved, they perceive not spirit manifest.

22 Spirit is spirit. It is the essence of self-knowledge. It knoweth itself and that which tormenteth it. It cometh into mortal flesh and saith, See that ye admit me.

23 I have knowledge of ether, now I take it into Form.

24 Is the spirit less of Spirit in that it betaketh it to Form? Is it not greater, that it seeketh such ennobling, confined in flesh to give tongue to its godhood? Is godhood an antic? I say it hath endurance, it arriveth at a stature, it cometh and goeth in and out of Form, it seeth its profit as vileness hath injured it.

25 Is a man a statue? is his corpse made of stone? hath the image-maker wrought it? can it know not any increase?

26 I tell you that the spirit of a man is the influence that he sheddeth; it is that which hath taken its presence from the Godhead and quickened itself in Form to know its own majesty.

27 Verily it happeneth unto each that is created.

28 How then say ye, that a spirit can enter into Form and become the thing called Man, and that never afterward there entereth more spirit, even my presence which is Form of the Father?

29 Can Spirit enter once and thereafter know palsy?

30 I tell you that Spirit entereth man continually, adding unto his stature, behold I give each spirit its increase.

31 I travel out to those who have entered my service, I dissolve into their essence, I give them my consciousness, I bathe them in my radiance.

32 Thereat do men say, Behold these are the Christlike! We perceive their vibrations! They bring us ennoblement!

33 Which one among you, being a father, departeth mortality and leaveth his children to fall into pits? Hath each father not his essence? yet doth he not cast vigilance over those whom he hath sired?

34 Love commandeth his spirit to watch over his offspring, to put words in their mouths which preserve them from follies.

35 Ever and anon he standeth at their shoulders, he entereth their hearts, he saith, Be circumspect! he guideth them to manners, he increaseth their stature.

36 Do the offspring always know that the parent hovereth over them? Not so, my beloved.

37 And if a father, being mortal, preserveth his offspring, how much more would I preserve those who are mine emissaries?

38 I say that I come unto those who have chosen me. I send them a pattern of that which is my personage. I make them as myself. I endow them with goodness. Their spirit presenteth me.

39 Whereof it is said of a man that the Christ is incarnate in him, that the Christ is reborn in one who cometh radiantly. I say, I am reborn hourly in those who make my music.

40 I preserve mine own majesty yet I share it with my cohorts. In that they are like unto me, their spirits take my pattern; I am in them and they are in me; behold we are one flesh, whereat the world exclaimeth saying, How can this thing be possible?

41 I say it is conversion that reacheth unto the spirit; it is the martyr's sacrifice; it is the seer's privilege; it happeneth unto those who take up my discipleship.

42 And yet do I repair into mine own being, I have my integrity, I preserve my own balance, I discern mine own watchfulness over myself.

43 As Spirit permeateth flesh, and men say, A child is born! so permeateth my Spirit the soul born of radiance that cometh on it suddenly.

44 Hath not my spirit talent to encompass many such? Say ye that I must confine myself to one instrument of personage? I say that is a sacrilege, I say it is a torment. For many behold my spirit descending and cry, Are these not false Christs who thus come to plague us?

45 My beloved, know the mystery. I come unto one who saileth far seas, behold I come as well to her with the broom in the cot of the lowly. I come unto the speaker who filleth many rostrums. I come unto the king and bid him know compassion. Think ye all marvels are the adversary's traffickings? How cometh it that men do say, Only the evil one performeth in wonders?

46 Be ye as adults, secure in maturity.

The above passage, chosen at random, is but one of hundreds which eloquently transport the questing soul. So what can one say about the *Golden Scripts?* That it is *The* Authority, the Authority by which all other authorities can be measured.

It is *The* Book of Wisdom, *The* Book of Truth, *the* living word as extolled by *The* Living Word. Beside it, all books of wisdom and truth pale in comparison, and no other living word can match it in eloquence, in wealth of startling truths, in mystical lyricism, in scope of vision, or in loftiness of Wisdom.

Its words, its overall attitude, its very mission, radiates Love. It has the tenderest, most heartwarming words of Love ever put into human language, English or otherwise. It radiates Love. And like the Bible, it can serve as a most potent tool of divination. One can open it randomly anytime one is perplexed, in need either of pertinent advice or personal comfort, or maybe just in need of a few moments in the most intimate presence of the wisest, the gentlest, and the most spiritually-evolved Being ever to don the costume of mortal earthling.

It is inconceivable to a brain stuffed with earthly trivia that such a repository of Love, good will, and Wisdom cannot be in wide print, especially in light of the vast metamorphoses that earth and her denizens are about to undergo in the near future. If ever the masses needed to have their consciousness raised by such a book, now would be the time for it.

To those with ears to hear, the *Golden Scripts* is at any time a refreshing sip of Spiritual spring water, a fulfilling and hearty snack of the bread of Wisdom. It is a bracing breath of mountain air, a mountain air washed with purest snow and scented with pine and spruce.

It is sanctuary. It is Love. It is Truth.

APPENDIX B: BENEDICTION

To that most enigmatic personage, the Apostle Paul, we owe our benediction, as given to us in his first epistle to the Thessalonians, verses 15-28:

"See that none render evil for evil unto any man; but ever follow that which is good, both among yourselves and to all men.

"Rejoice evermore. Pray without ceasing. In all things give thanks: for this is the will of God in Christ Jesus concerning you.

"Quench not the Spirit. Despise not prophesyings. Prove all things; hold fast that which is good.

"Abstain from all appearance of evil.

"And the very God of peace sanctify you wholly; and I pray God your whole spirit and soul and body be preserved blameless unto the coming of our Lord Jesus Christ.

"Faithful is he that calleth you, who also will do it.

"Brethren, pray for us. Greet all the brethren with an holy kiss.

"I charge you by the Lord that this epistle be read unto all the holy brethren.

"The grace of our Lord Jesus Christ be with you.

"So be it. So be it. *SO BE IT!*"

APPENDIX C: MANIFESTO

You who have stayed with us this far are, by your own choosing, among the Select Few. More about that organization later.

By having come this far, and by having understood and somewhat believed what you have just read, you have marked yourselves as being here on Earth in service to the race. For you must easily understand, by all means, that there are many people among us who cannot comprehend nor accept these things in the way they have been presented within this one brief book. It is therefore your task to convince as many of these stragglers as possible of the eternal impact of the Highest Truth: Unity.

Go and present this philosophy to all whom you truly care for: to parents, to brothers and sisters, to children — *especially* to children — to distant relatives and close friends and casual acquaintances, and to enemies, and to all to whom you are led. And *live* the doctrine; live it so that they to whom you would present it can see its Wisdom and its efficacy.

For you see, it is quite simple: unless you can qualify the unaware souls for passengership aboard a rescuing UFO, or better yet, help them to awaken in flesh, we are going to lose them. They will perish in their current physical form even as the Earth perishes in its current physical form and is transposed to a physical form in a higher dimension. For the Earth is *evolving*, and those who cannot evolve with it must of necessity be left behind. They may incarnate again on another time/space planet at Earth's old level, or they may resume their incarnations again on the New Earth. But they will not be saved by the Rainbow Bridge which links the old to the new, as will you and others who can understand and practice the inescapable Truth of Unity.

Among Earth's hordes, the Jews are deserving of special attention, for they are indeed a Breed apart. They are the remnants, you see, of those who failed the prior Harvest of Souls. Some of them were too attached to earthlife and its pleasures, or to their small selves, or both, to venture onto the rescue vessels for the final farewell to our Blue Star, while others were yet so barbaric as to be fearful of the highly different beings who taught love and respect and adoration of the One God. And being fearful, they foolishly fled their would-be saviors.

But the last message the Jews were given as they were unavoidably left behind was that they must maintain racial purity, for they would have another opportunity for salvation in a future life on Earth, when their Messiah would come to restore them to their True Kingdom. The message referred of course to Man's True Estate, the Heavenly Kingdom of the Father, but the Jews — who are now the oldest and most advanced race on Earth — confused and elaborated on this promise over the years until it became a belief in some form of earthly kingdom, one in which God's chosen people might even reign supreme over their fellows. And oddly enough, this is what has indeed come to pass since the advent some 20 centuries ago of their Messiah, for having dwelt on Earth the longest, the Jews are preeminent in the arts and sciences and letters, and they cherish their preeminence — even those among them who are humble servants of Man and who so willingly share their talents for the uplifting of Mankind. Let these people know that their hard-won earthly preeminence is but a shadow compared to the glories they attain when they sacrifice the petty self to the All Highest Father and dedicate the small will to the Will for the All Highest Good!

For the Jewish Messiah did indeed make an advance appearance to his flock, and as did many of us non-Jews, they did, many of them, reject his most True and Wise and Loving message. Yet many of the more humble Jews also accepted the message, in spite of the fact that it held out no hope of true superiority over any of their fellow men. Israel must indeed humble Herself, and accept the Reality of Unity and the behavior It counsels, as displayed and told to Earth by Jesus of Nazareth during his mission of mercy.

Jesus of Nazareth is indeed the Jews' true Messiah of legend, the leader of the Christ Force which shepherds the well-being of Earth and her children. He will again lead the fleet of rescue vessels. He will again give the Jews and all other prisoners of Earth the opportunity to follow their True Light — their Christ Light — instead of remaining on Earth or an old Earth counterpart for yet another lengthy round of decay and death. He and his emissaries will speak to Earth's minions in each of their languages, but the message will be the same: the Unity in Spirit of All That Is. And those with ears to hear shall number themselves among the chosen.

You, the reader of these Truths, can serve in the advance guard of the Christ Force by getting these simple facts across to as many loved ones as you can. You may not be their last chance, but you may indeed be their *best* chance. By serving thus, you are denoted as a member of the Select Few. The Select Few is a celestial service organization which indeed *is* an advance guard, on Earth, for the Christ Force. You are joyous participants of the Harvest, and you are indeed a highly privileged few. The glories you will reap from your service are of a magnitude not capably borne by the human mind, so it is pointless to attempt their description.

The Select Few is commissioned, and It is commissioned by a Most High Source. Therefore do its members know divine protection at all times, in all that they undertake. You can move fearlessly and confidently in any direction your Light guides you. For you are servants of a most Mighty Order, the Christ Force. You glory in even the most minute effort that you make on behalf of that Force. Being aware of the One, you know that any effort put forth on behalf of another being is an effort for your own True Self.

I am not given to know the size of the Select Few's constituency. Its ranks could number 10 or 10 million. The Select Few's name derives from the fact that Its members are few indeed in comparison to Earth's existing hordes, and in comparison to the enormous amount of work to be done. Therefore, the Harvest will not be an easy one.

Those of you who venture forth to work among the Jews, especially if you were born of that race yourself, should be aware that your commission is indeed the most glorious of all, demanding of the best and most highly qualified candidates. For were lesser members to be assigned to this squadron, they would be intellectually torn asunder. You will encounter enormous hostility, as would anyone else approaching that race with a message containing any reference to *Christ*. But be aware that your message is a True One, of the Highest Truths, and a Wise One, of the Highest Wisdom, and that he who has Right on his side is thrice-armed.

"And where two or more go forth together in my name, there go the forces of mighty armies, armies of Spirit and Intellect and Form. And they shall overcome any obstacle placed before them, even one honed and fashioned over countless generations. For the Truth shall set men free. And the free shall return to rescue their former fellow captives of flesh."